Return
YOUR PATH TO
LASTING CHANGE

RETURN
Your Path to Teshuvah
© Tziporah Heller
2015

First edition August 2015

All rights reserved.

Printed in Israel

hellersite.contact@gmail.com

Distributor in Israel:
hellersite.contact@gmail.com

Distributor in the United States:

 MENUCHA
PUBLISHERS

Menucha Publishers Inc.
1235 38th street
Brooklyn N.Y. 11218

Graphic Design: Aviad Ben Simon

ISBN: 978-1-4951-7254-0

Return

YOUR PATH TO
LASTING CHANGE

"This time things will be different..."

Rebbetzin
Tziporah Heller

Dedicated in Memory of:

Frederick H. Mayer OBM, 12 Tammuz

Erika Neter Mayer OBM, 9 Tammuz

Marx Maier OBM, 2 Elul

Bertha Rothschild Maier OBM, 9 Elul

Emil Neter OBM, 16 Tammuz

Hedwig Caroline Neter OBM, 2 Sivan

Fred Neter OBM, Rosh Chodesh Iyar

Ruth Maier Kohn OBM, 2 Adar

*May their dear souls
rest in gan eden*

לעילוי נשמת

נפתלי בן מרדכי ז"ל – י"ב תמוז

אריקה אוגוסטה בת **ברוך** ז"ל – ט' תמוז

מרדכי בן יעקב ז"ל – ב' אלול

בעסלה שרה בת **וולף שמעון** ז"ל – ט' אלול

ברוך בן אלי ז"ל – ט"ו תמוז

הדוויג קרוליין בת **לודוויג** ז"ל – ב' סיון

פרד בן ברוך ז"ל – ר"ח אייר

רוס בת **מרדכי** ז"ל – ב' אדר

ת נ צ ב " ה

Contents

ACKNOWLEDGEMENTS

No one knows better than I do how easy it is to give up. Changing anything is, by the nature of things, a challenge. When it comes to making genuine and enduring changes in yourself, without G-d's help, it is virtually impossible. In His unending compassion, G-d opens the door for true change and return to the potential within each one of us at specific times of the year. Elul, the Days of Repentance and Yom Kippur, are treasures. These are days of awe, love and, most of all, opportunity.

You are not alone in your search. In this handbook, you will find ideas from some of the deepest thinkers and greatest Jewish sages. I have done my best to make their words accessible to you so that they can speak to you with the clarity and depth that I found them speaking to me.

The process began with Julia Cook transcribing *shiurim*. My dear, dear friends, Rachel Greenblatt and Debby Howarth, have been with me every step of the way in turning the *shiurim* into a handbook. Rachel transformed the transcriptions into a book and meticulously reviewed every sentence. Debby Howarth did the task of taking my "I'm pretty sure Maharal said this in *Netiv HaAvodah*" and turning my hazy references (or even less) into accurate source citations. My family encouraged me, supported me and helped me in every conceivable way. Both you and I owe them thanks for making these ideas available to you.

Hashem has given me the opportunity to learn and to teach, for which I will never stop thanking Him. My late husband, Rav Dovid, *zatzal*, was never afraid to let me blossom. He encouraged me to teach whoever would learn, and to follow the dictate of the Sages, to "learn what your heart desires." He kept me on track, and presented me with a living example of everything that I saw in print. It is to him that I dedicate this handbook.

FOREWORD

Hashem presents you with the possibilities of living a life in which you are really alive, or choosing to live a life in which you are dead.

The classical definition of death is that nothing at all in someone's body still functions. Spiritual death takes place when nothing is moving forward spiritually. Look back at your life - so many changes take place in early childhood. The difference between a fifteen-year-old and a twenty-five-year-old is also vast. Is there always that much change that takes place between the ages of thirty-five and forty-five? Odds are you have made many of the life decisions that define your life from the outside. You may have married, began your family, and are already established in your career. What are your plans for the next forty or so years? More of the same? You may be asking "Why not? If I am happy, why keep on making changes?" This way of thinking takes you to spiritual death. Some people stop "living" far earlier....

Discontent isn't the same as growth. You don't have to be unhappy in order to want to move further. When you go back to your childhood, you may remember how happy you were with each new barrier you were able to knock down. Going to school yourself, choosing your own clothes, learning how to work a computer or to drive were marvelous moments, weren't they? You are programmed for self-actualization. In fact, so is everything else on the planet. There aren't any birds who can fly who select not to, or any plants that just don't feel like photosynthesizing.

The Torah tells you that G-d wants you to choose life. It also tells you to choose blessing over curse. The simplest meaning of the word "blessing" is wishing someone well. This isn't the entire story. The root letters of the word brachah ברכה (blessing) are beit (2) ב, reish (200) ר and chaf (20) כ. Each letter is the first expansion of its unit.

Two is the first number that goes beyond one, twenty, the first expansion of the tens, and two hundred the first expansion of the hundreds.

Being blessed means being more.

The way the Torah presents you with the instruction to choose uses the word Re'eh, which means See! In the singular. Alsheich points out that the reason for this is that unlike an earthly ruler, Hashem is concerned with the inner reality of each of us, not just that "the work gets done" in the broadest sense. One of the problems that some of you face when you are making your way in the Great World, is that you may feel rather invisible. You go to work or to school, attend shul on Shabbos or not, and no one else seems to be affected one way or the other. The people around you may even invite you for Shabbos or a holiday, but if you can't make it, you don't get the feeling that they missed anything really important.

You are wrong.

When Hashem created vegetation, He made innumerable blades of grass. Each one of them has an angel that stands above it and tells it to grow. Each one of the billions of ants has its own message (those of you who are familiar with Perek Shirah, the nature song, will even know what its message is!). Humans are far more unique than anything else in nature is. Your face isn't identical with anyone else's face (even if you are a twin). The inner world that you live in is equally as unique. That's why Hashem began creating humans by forming one individual, not an entire human population. There are roads that only you will walk, choices that only you will make. You are part of a community that is broader and more eternal than the specific "hood" you live in. The give and take of being part of the Jewish People is an indelible part of your identity.

When you go to shul, accept an invitation, maintain your ethical principles and standards in the workplace or in school; you are becoming a living blessing. You are affecting the people around you whether they are sensitive enough to feel it overtly, or whether the effect is too subtle for them to recognize it at the time.

You are a giver, even when you think that you are forced by your life circumstances into being the eternal taker. There will be other times when you feel that you are overwhelmed by people and their Needs and their Issues. That means, for the moment at least, that you are in a different role, and have to tap into a different way of drawing down the blessing that your situation opens up to you.

A well-known song was composed around one of Rebbe Nachman's works (In Lekutei Moharan 2:11 and 63).

Know that each shepherd has his own niggun;

And each blade of grass has its own song;

From the song of the grass, the shepherd's niggun is made…

How beautiful it is to hear their song;

To pray with them and serve Hashem with joy;

And from the song of the grass, who sings with purity and no thought of reward;

Your heart is filled with song and yearns;

For Eretz Yisrael, and awakens its light and draws it to you.

Enjoy your blessing, choose it and do not be afraid or alone. You never really are, and it is time that you let that realization touch you.

Tziporah Heller

Jerusalem, Elul 5775

OVERVIEW OF TIME

Time Itself Is a Creation

The first principle to bear in mind when starting the process of Teshuvah is that time itself is a creation. Time is the progression of change. Hashem made the world in order for us to measure change, as the Torah says: "The reason Hashem made the luminaries, the sun and the moon, was to allow for the possibility of us noticing the progression of time."[1]

How Does Time Work?

The sun and moon allow you to measure time. The Torah tells you that the reason G-d gave you a way of measuring time is to allow you to use the unique nature of every moment, day and month to take notice of *otot and mo'adim* – which means "signs and times of meeting." The energy of each month is different. Each has its own prevailing astral body. We notice the shifting of the months through the waxing and waning of the moon which is a sign for us to observe the different spiritual capacities and to allow them to flourish in the appropriate month.

The fact that we count twelve months is far from random. There are twelve different ways of arranging Hashem's name, *yud-kay-vav-kay*. In many siddurim, after Hallel or in the prayers of Mussaf for Rosh Chodesh, an excerpt from the *Sefer Bnei Yissachar*,[2] can be found which provides a brief description of these concepts. I am not a kabbalist, but the letters of His Name tell you the path you can follow to reach Him every month. Knowing this helps you to develop a different relationship to the passage of time.

---

1 *Bereishit, 1:14*
2 Written by Rabbi Tzvi Elimelech Spira of Dinov (c. 1783–1841), also called the "*Bnei Yisaschar*" after his classic work of this name;

The Hebrew name of the month also gives you a handle on the month's inner dimensions. The way you can seek Hashem in Tishrei is different from the way in which you would seek Him during Elul, and both are different from that of Av. The astral sign is meant to give you a hint of how you can accomplish this. The word *mo'ed* means "holiday," as in Chol Hamo'ed, but its literal meaning is "a time of meeting." It is the root of the word *va'ad*, which means "committee." Every month provides us with a different form of meeting point in your connection to Hashem.

The Nature of Elul

The astral sign of Elul is the Virgin.

Step back from yourself. Open your heart to Elul by being (at least for the moment) a young, idealistic woman who is still yearning for the completion of giving yourself, surrendering yourself to your beloved one. This is the heart of Elul: [*bitul*, which is a homonym of the word *betulah*] opening up, making yourself vulnerable by surrendering to the One you love, and in the process, becoming more than what you are now.

Step back enough to silence your "I" – the part of you that says, "I need"; "I am"; and "I want." Focus instead on "You." Elul can free you to experience the kind of yearning that leads you to move with trust toward the "other."

Practical Tips for Coming Closer to Hashem in Elul

In order for us to be able to move into this energy, we need to abide by specific practices:

1. Give more tzedakah than you normally give – 'Lose more' materially to gain more spiritually.

A small amount is enough, just as long as it is a bit *more* than you usually give. A few coins at every tefillah can make a huge difference in your perspective. Do you have an emotional relationship to money? Welcome to the club. This is the reason the Torah calls money *damim*, which means "blood." One example is where the phrase *damim yeshalem*[3] is used. It's meaning, in context, is to pay financial damages. Its literal meaning is to "pay blood." This is why people – even well balanced, sane people – can get so caught up in quibbling with a taxi driver over a few shekalim, even if they earn $180 an hour.

Therefore, whenever you give tzedakah monetarily you *do* always lose materially. However, when you choose to 'lose more' materially, you are confronting your fears of becoming 'less', and are challenged to trust that Hashem will make sure your needs are met overall, even if you cannot see how this is so. This strengthens your ability to give and trust, which is the work of Elul. This can expand your sense of self. You can become more spiritually real and actualized.

The more often you reach out and give to another Jew, the more you will become attached to the collective soul of *Klal Yisrael* (the entire Jewish People). The most meaningful surrender to the Will of Hashem is as a people, not as individuals, because we are not islands, but rather we are part of something greater than ourselves. Tzedakah opens this door.

2. Reciting *Tehillim* – Psalm 27 twice a day for forty days.

This psalm is one that hints, not just at Elul but at all the holy days that will be coming, namely Rosh Hashanah, Yom Kippur and Sukkot, as significant times of *mo'ed*. The goal is to say it twice a day for forty days.

The *Zohar* says that just the act of saying *Tehillim* has a huge impact on you. Its power stems from the spiritual force of its author.[4] King David had a universal soul. He is described as having a soul that was a spark of Adam HaRishon's soul. Adam was the source of humankind and therefore is described as being a "collective soul," since he is the root of all future humans. He gave seventy years of his life to David, who inherited the collective nature of Adam's soul.[5]

Many people want to say *Tehillim* but don't feel they can actually

---

3 *Shemot, 22:2*
4 *Zohar 1:39b; regarding King David composing Tehillim with prophetic vision;*
5 *Zohar 1:168b;*

do it because they don't understand Hebrew (or, in the days before Artscroll's translations were popularized, find the English so different from their normal way of speaking that it seems like *Tehillim* must have been composed by Sir Walter Scott). Obviously, the more you understand what you are saying, the better it is, but even if you cannot completely grasp it, saying it still has a very deep and profound effect. The main *kavanah*, intention, of this chapter of *Tehillim* is: "*There is one thing I want from Hashem and that is what I am asking for, to dwell in Hashem's house (to be surrounded by awareness of Hashem) all the days of my life, to gaze at the pleasantness of Hashem and to visit His sanctuary*".[6]

King David was referring to the Beit HaMikdash, but he never lived to see it. You and the Psalmist both know on the deepest level that the amount of your G-d-consciousness, clarity and joy coming from being your highest self, is what being a servant of Hashem means. This chapter tells you that faith in its highest sense is possible; that you can overcome your impediments and that you believe that Hashem can help you.

Do it now! Open up your Tehillim to chapter 27. Read it slowly, after each line, ask yourself, "What does this have to do with me?"

3. Receiving and giving forgiveness.

Elul is called "*Chodesh Harachamim V'haSelichot, The Month of Mercy and Forgiveness.*" Immediately after doing your *cheshbon hanefesh*, you need to start working on your list of people from whom you need to ask forgiveness. *This is a crucial step before you begin delving into the broader and more general, and therefore lengthier and more complex, aspects of teshuvah.*

---

6 *Tehillim* 27:4;

SHIUR 1

The Four Parts to *Cheshbon Hanefesh*:

Part 1: Examine each era of your life.

Take about twenty minutes a day during the first few days of Elul and use it to change your entire future. Examine your early childhood, your adolescence, early adulthood, the first half of your twenties, the second half of your twenties, and so on. Then break down each era into the events that you remember. The more detailed you can be in doing this, the more real your *cheshbon hanefesh* is going to be. It is not enough to simply leave your description of your adolescence as "I went to school." You need to try to recall who your friends were; what the major events that occurred during that period were; who your teachers were and what your relationship to them was like; what was going on at home; what your relationship was like with your parents and siblings.

This should be done without any judgment. This means that you do not try to assess whether a certain occurrence was good or bad, or try to apportion blame. Just focus on what happened.

Try to write this in outline form so that you can refer to it later, which will make it easier to you. Don't try to write an entire diary. Memory is selective, and there is no way of knowing whether what you remember is what you need to remember, which is why you need to do this every year. Your feelings about what you did will also change from year to year.

There are people who are self-developed enough to be able to go through the four parts of *cheshbon hanefesh* every night and analyse the current day every day of their lives. They do not go through the whole year every night.

Part 2: Examine your responses.

Ask yourself how you responded to what was going on around you. What were the choices you made? How did you respond after choosing? In school, were you active or passive? Did you do your homework? Did you have friends? Did you try to have friends? Try to assess exactly what was going on. Again, this must be done without judgment, because most likely you were doing whatever you felt you had to do for your own good at the time.

Part 3: Examine your choices.

Ask yourself which choices got you closer to who and where you want to be, and which got you further away from your real life goals. Don't try to analyze why those decisions were made or whose fault it was that you reacted in the way you did. Just assess whether they brought you closer or further.

> An example of this from my own life, is where I did as little in school as I could *because I could get away with it.* I got good marks without any effort. Did this get me closer to my goals? Sort of. I learned to prioritize though this, but I didn't always use my time wisely. Questions such as "Why wasn't I engaged in schoolwork?" or "Why wasn't it interesting enough to hold my attention?" are unimportant.

Part 4: What were your thought processes?

a) "When I made bad choices, what was I thinking and feeling?"

b) "When I made good choices, what was I thinking and feeling?"

If you can answer these questions, you really know who you are on the inside. You know your thought patterns and will be able to analyze them. Once you know yourself on the inside, then you have a *cheshbon hanefesh*. A *cheshbon hanefesh* is like an inventory. An inventory not only looks at what is lacking or defective, it also takes note of what you have. Therefore, you will find that you have visible testimony to your good choices, not just your bad choices. You will be able to recognize your patterns of making good choices, as well as your patterns of making bad choices.

Returning to Your Higher Self

Your goal in Teshuvah is to return to your higher and better self, and the method you can use is ridding yourself of the impediments. These are blocks constructed by your less-developed self. While doing this, you will discover that both your good and bad feelings are usually coming from the same source. Your bad choices and feelings are directed one way, and your good choices and feelings are being directed a different way.

You therefore need to focus on determining what your motivations were when you were making your choices, as this will help you to figure out the middah that is attached to those choices, and consequently, what to work on. But, *it is important to note that the name of the force that moved you towards directing your feelings and choices to the bad places is* **Yetzer Hara**. *The feelings themselves are not the problem. The direction they went is.*

If you are a Ba'alat Teshuvah, then you must remember that when you are evaluating your past choices, keep in mind that you were doing what was best for you at the time. There is therefore no reason to assume that you have to do Teshuvah on choices that were the best of what was accessible to you in the past. Of course, now that you have done Teshuvah you will see that those choices that you realized were bad for you are the ones that you chose to change. You can also take choices that were totally outside of your reality off the guilt list. They are finished and you no longer have to revisit them. The only places that you have to revisit are places that are in your present.

> Again, I will use myself as an example. I am an idealistic person. This means that if I believe in something, I will go for it. My worst trait is that I do not carefully examine whether I have ego involvement in what I choose. Both of these outcomes stem from the same root of my wanting to choose what is right. Teshuvah here would mean sticking to ideals that are true and eliminating the ego-obstacles of the *yetzer hara.*

Another illustration of this can be culled from my experience of going to seminary in Israel, and being in Eretz Yisrael for the first time. In those days, they did not have computerized means of researching background as thoroughly as they do today. On the second morning after my arrival, I had my interview with the principal, Rav Wolf, *zatzal*. He was to determine to which of the two seminary classes he would assign me: "*Hei One*" or "*Hei Two*," and he also wanted to get to know me. At that point all he knew was that I had just come fresh from Bais Yaakov.

My high school, Bais Yaakov of Crown Heights, had a policy of sending the girls for the last year to Williamsburg. This meant that I was coming straight from Bais Yaakov of Williamsburg, a Yiddish-speaking mini-world in the midst of the ethnic kaleidoscope of Brooklyn. My family background was different with a capital D. My parents were American-born and very much part of their generation. They were children of immigrants, and took pride in their social and economic integration with the greater society. My grandmother was Yiddish speaking, and a whisper of her culture was part of the backdrop of our home.

Besides seeing my report card, all Rav Wolf really knew about me was that I spoke and understood Yiddish and English and had just gotten off the plane. So, he spoke to me in Yiddish. I answered him in a rather strange patois of broken classical Hebrew, thinking: "*I won't speak to the Rav in the language of the Diaspora*," and I continued the conversation in this way. If this were to happen today, it's likely that I would have been asked to leave the school.

Nothing could have been further from Bnei Brak's view of the "New Jew" than my language preference seemed to indicate. It was not so simple to send me back home in those days: it was inconceivable. Although he might possibly have suggested that I try somewhere else, he went for another option. He thought for a while, then answered me in Ivrit, saying, "You can go wherever you want to go in the dormitories, and you can even read whatever you want to read. I will never ask you to account for anything, but *don't take anyone with you*." I was accepted on that basis.

This shows two things about me: first, that my extreme idealism was quite misguided at the time, and second, that that kind of idealism can very easily slide into chutzpah and *gaavah*!

Each of you will discover a different pattern. This means that no one's Teshuvah will look like anyone else's, because their inventories are not the same.

Forgiveness

Some of your choices will have involved damaging or hurting other people. Your next step therefore, is to make a list of people from whom you will have to ask forgiveness. How to do this will soon be discussed.

There is a lot of room for denial and blame while doing this, but you need to move away from this (and sacrifice the good feeling of "I'm alright; you aren't alright" that this kind of thinking evokes) because it does not have much to do with Teshuvah.

What you should be trying to do here is assess whether the interaction with the person you hurt took you closer or further from where you want to be, both with them and as a person. It doesn't matter why it happened or what the other person's role is/was. It is simply about how you want to take responsibility for playing your role in your script. Ultimately it is one that you are still in the process of writing.

Asking for Forgiveness. Writing the list may be painful, but it has to be real. List all the people you damaged, either emotionally, financially or spiritually. The next step is to ask their forgiveness, which is of course extremely difficult (and in some cases agonizing) if you are speaking about big things. There is a big difference between apologizing for spilling soup on someone's shirt and asking someone to forgive you for always placing them in your shadow.

Your goal when asking for forgiveness. You have to recognize that whenever you harm another person, you diminish her self-esteem. When a person is hurt, she feels vulnerable and robbed of her strength and ability. Your goal, therefore, is to build her up and make her feel able to undo the damage that you did to her emotionally. (Whether you can undo damage you caused financially or physically will have to be determined by a different set of parameters.)

Being honest with yourself. You therefore need to be honest with yourself. Most people don't get up in the morning with the intention to go out and harm someone. Most of us are reactive. This means that you are likely to have said something nasty to the other person because you felt as though she had hurt or attacked you. It is very tempting to say, "I am so sorry for saying this and this and that," and then hinting or saying overtly that "it was because of you and what you did."

Taking care of yourself. Your job is to take care of YOU. If the other person agrees with what you've said, and responds, "You're right, I'm sorry," that's lovely. If you say, "You are absolutely right, I never should have said that," that is good too.

What if she says, "It's about time you said something. You really were wrong," and then takes no responsibility for her part in the painful interaction in which you both took part? Your goal is not to change the other person. Your goal is to build the other person by removing the harm you did.

What if you don't think you can accomplish this goal in a face-to-face confrontation? What if you are afraid the other person will react defensively and reactivate the old argument? If so, don't confront her in person. Send an email, or leave a message on the phone when you know she isn't home. Do it in a way that is not interactive. A side benefit to this approach is that people do read their emails, and they do listen to phone messages and they do so in a way that is not interrupted. This is by no means the best way to accomplish your goal, but it is often the only way to achieve anything that even remotely resembles real healing.

Suffering humiliation may be your ticket to Olam Habah. If the person responds to this approach by asking to meet you in person to discuss this, what she is saying, in effect, is that she needs to make you feel bad about this. She feels so diminished by what you did that she cannot be satisfied with you simply leaving things with you in the higher position and her below. Here you will need to tell yourself again and again that suffering humiliation in this sense – *l'Shem Shamayim*, could be your ticket to *Olam Habah*.

Paying back whatever you owe. If you caused someone physical or financial damage, you owe her compensation. Just saying, "I am so sorry that I lied to you when I told you that I knew you would not be eligible for a mortgage that would give you terms you could live with. The truth is that I really had my eye on that house, and as you know I bought it," is very nice…if what you are after is catharsis.

If your action resulted in an actual financial loss, you would have to consult with a Rav before you face this person and question whether there is any amount of money you could offer her as compensation. In this way, when you approach her you can say at the outset, "I spoke with Rabbi X (preferably someone whom she would feel comfortable consulting), who suggested that I give you this sum of money."

However, if the amount in question is significant (either actually or emotionally) you would be far better off saying, "Let's consult with Rabbi X about what I should do." If, in fact, you and your friend see the situation differently, Rabbi X would not be able to render an opinion at all without hearing both sides fully.

What if you can't find that person? If you find yourself in a position where you can't find the person you harmed, you first need to be honest with yourself as to whether it is genuinely impossible, or whether it simply requires a great deal of effort on your part. Sometimes just networking will do it. Other times you may have to be willing to make more of an effort.

If you genuinely can't find the person you need to repay, you are in a different situation. You can't recompense the person you harmed, but neither are you allowed to gain from your dishonest or morally dubious deed. The basic rule is that you need to bring the positive side of whatever you took away from the world when you hurt that person, back into the world. If you can't return money that you received dishonestly, give that amount to a public charity that will help make the world a better place. Who knows? One day your victim may also benefit from this *tikkun*.

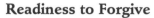

Readiness to Forgive

There will be those who come to ask you for forgiveness. Be ready to forgive them. You can do this by separating the consequences of their choices from their choices.

How can you do this? Rambam tells us in Hilchot Teshuvah that you need to be in the right frame of mind in order for this to work effectively. Essentially, your mindset should be that you realize that the consequences of all actions come from Hashem, while the choice whether or not to do the action came from the person who is asking your forgiveness. If the person regrets her choice, then that is really all she can do.

Consequences, for instance, are what you would endure if someone deliberately gave you bad advice for purposes of their own gain, but you must realize that you were never meant to have that gain. Otherwise, Hashem would have foiled their schemes.

I spent an unforeseen three-hour layover in London and missed my connecting flight to Dallas. What made it more frustrating was that the airline rep had told me that the plane was still at the gate when I arrived, but it would be too late to board by the time we passengers could get to where we needed to be. I could easily have fallen into the trap of blame/anger/negativity. Although I can't say that this is always how I respond to this sort of situation, this time I took some control over my mind.

I asked myself, "How would Reb Aryeh Levine, the well-known tzaddik of Yerushalayim have responded?" He certainly suffered ample frustration in the course of his life! I thought, "He would have looked around to examine what real possibilities were open to him." I looked around me and noticed that two Israeli women were in the same boat, with one critical exception; they didn't speak or understand English. I had the opportunity to help them navigate immigration (which in England can be very tricky) and find their new gate.

This did not mean that the airline was taking responsibility for seeing that its passengers were treated with respect or even basic honesty…the flight could have been held up for a few more minutes, or compensation could have been offered for their tardiness. It did mean that I could resist the temptation to think that I was somehow belittling the airline's ineptitude by using the afternoon constructively. G-d offered me an opportunity, so I took it! This has nothing to do with the ethical issues that the airline was unwilling to deal with.

The Process of Teshuvah

Teshuvah entails a minimum of three steps, but it sometimes requires as many as five.

Teshuvah means "return"; its goal is to return you to your higher self. You now know who your higher self is thanks to your examination of the thoughts and feelings you had when you made good choices and the very fact that you made good choices. Even though the main goal of Teshuvah is to focus on the thoughts and feelings that include changing your character traits and your belief system, as will be explained in depth later on, you have to start with action.

The Talmud tells us that an angel taught you Torah before your birth.[1] You can rediscover this Torah. It is embedded in your subconscious. When you do Teshuvah, you can move toward returning to this pristine state of being. Getting to know yourself deeply, and acting on what you discover about yourself, is necessary for two reasons: first, actions affect thought; second, you can see what your middot are through your actions.

Actions affect thoughts. When you begin by trying to isolate the negative traits that trigger the wrong actions and those traits have been part of you for as long as you can remember, it may just be too hard. You have built-in defenses, just like the rest of us. Sefer haChinuch tells us (mitzvah 16) that even the Torah prohibition of not breaking the bones of the Pesach offering changes the way you think and feel. Your external actions mold and shape your internal emotions more deeply than you realize at the time.

---

1 *Talmud Bavli, Niddah 30b;*

An example of this would be someone who is fine with buying stolen goods. This is one of the actions that Rambam[2] tells us that can even cut you off from your inherent ability to experience the portion of Olam Habah that was set aside for you. If this has been the way she "shops" since she was a teen, she does not feel guilty, so her first step would be to change the deed. This, in turn, will sensitize her to other people and their feeling of being invaded when a thief victimizes them. It is HaShem's Divine providence that gives you what you need to live your life and succeed in your mission in this world. You never "need" to steal.

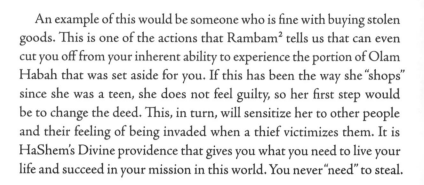

The first time Liora bought a music disk near Jaffa Gate, she should have thought about how they managed to offer the latest frum music at half the price the stores in Geulah would have charged. She had accustomed herself to never asking too many questions. Why wonder whether it's alright to ask a child to tell the ticket inspector that he is four when he is closer to six? Why ask whether giving an out-of-town address to avoid paying tax is really honest? These questions were no longer relevant to Liora. She felt no guilt, experienced no conflict. In fact, if a friend were to say something even remotely critical of this sort of "shtick," she would have made the friend feel as though she was living in the wrong century. Liora now knows the reason why. Dishonesty wasn't something she did; at that point, it was something she was.

It is crucial to work from the outside-in, starting from your external actions, even though your goal is to change the inside. But if you focus only on the outside and never get to the inside, you will find yourself in a situation that is analogous to cutting weeds, instead of uprooting them. You need to begin by identifying and doing away with the weeds themselves.

---

2 Hilchot Teshuvah

Make a Realistic Plan for the Future

Take it gradually, step by step as follows:

1. *Viduy*. This is the "confession" you say five times on Yom Kippur. The purpose of the confession is to make you aware of the deeds, which can inform you what the middot are, so that you can ask Hashem to erase the damage that these deeds did to you. It is therefore imperative for you to go through lists from your *cheshbon hanefesh*. You can go through the davening for Yom Kippur Katan, if you have that. There are Yom Kippur Katan booklets available in English and you will see there the long *Viduy* of Rav Nissim Gaon, which is more exhaustive than the *Ashamnu, bagadnu* and the *Al Cheit*.

If this isn't an option for you, either because it isn't available to you or you find it too overwhelming, then you can stick with the *Viduy* of *Ashamnu Bagadnu*. We will not deal with this in detail here, as there is already extensive literature on this subject available elsewhere.

There are two elements that you need to be clear on.

a) *See the deed as an impediment*. The purpose isn't to focus on how terrible you are but to see this deed as an impediment and to recognize it as such.

b) *Acknowledge that you are dealing with it*. Know that Hashem, because He is so enormously kind, will erase the damage that you have done to yourself. Therefore, the more detailed your *Viduy* is, the more effective it will be, because the more honestly you confront the barriers that keep you away from being your highest self, the more likely it is that you will actually change.

Once you have gone through the Yom Kippur Katan booklet, go through the *cheshbon hanefesh* in your mind and think about it at least briefly. Think about the implications of this for you, not just for the other person, if indeed there was another person involved.

In Teshuvah nothing is irrevocable.

The value of this can be seen through analyzing the middah of avoidance. You could make demands of yourself and because of this you could honestly say that you never daven with *kavanah*. Your *Viduy* will then include this. You will acknowledge that you have the opportunity to connect with Hashem and you aren't doing it. Once you *say* that this is the case, there is something that you can do about it.

It is like getting a diagnosis from a doctor. Even though a person who gets a terrible diagnosis could burst into tears, nobody will say "…therefore don't get a diagnosis." A person might burst into tears over a negative diagnosis because she feels the consequences of this diagnosis in terms of how it will affect her life expectancy or the possibility of her suffering. These outcomes are irrevocable, but in Teshuvah nothing is irrevocable. The damage is there whether you confront it or not, but Teshuvah makes it possible for you to get rid of the layers of damage and callousness that may have been your self-definition, and may have caused you to do untold harm to yourself and to others. Therefore, Teshuvah should always be accompanied by a certain feeling of relief and simchah.

2. *Regret.* This means recognizing that the deed was harmful – harmful to you and to the world, in that it made the world a darker place; and possibly harmful to another person. Recognizing that the deed is harmful is the key to not repeating that deed. This means letting go of whatever emotional pay-off you were getting by doing the wrong thing.

It is important that you do not fall into the trap of blame. You should not become absorbed in placing blame on yourself, on your own nature or on somebody else, because as soon as you assign blame, you cannot feel regret. The deed is not your fault; it's the fault of the school system, society, your mother, whoever, and therefore it is not something that you need to concern yourself about.

Even though most of our actions are triggered by external factors, the person who is ultimately held accountable for them is you. You are the proud owner of whatever damage your bad thoughts bring about. Therefore, you have to feel authentic regret for the damage you caused.

3. *Changing behaviors.* The last stage in this process is to adopt different behaviors for the future. In order to accomplish this, you need to have some sort of a plan: what exactly you need to do and how you can go about achieving this goal. Saying things like "From now on I will never be escapist," or, "From now on I will be completely honest with myself," is not going to work.

Methods of Doing Teshuvah

You can make a realistic plan for the future in several ways. The following method is based on Rambam's method for Teshuvah[3].

Visualize a better version of the event. Once you have isolated your thoughts and feelings, and the deeds that come from them, you need to picture your worst moment. Take yourself back to that place mentally. Focus on details, such as where you were in the room, who was there and what damage was done. Then replay the scene in your mind, but instead of imagining it as it really occurred, try to picture it as you wish it had actually played out. You are taking yourself to the opposite extreme now. This leaves a huge gap between these two visualizations.

In order to be able to reach this ideal, you need to take tiny steps that will narrow the gap between these extremes. It is easy to tell yourself that these little steps cannot possibly help, so why bother – but the truth is that they help cumulatively. It is also possible to tell yourself, "But this might take me a year!" - Which is fine. What is important is that you actually begin the process.

An example of this would be to look at your family life and see where you made many mistakes involving self-absorption. You then picture the opposite extreme of this with you being kinder and more respectful. Ask yourself, "What is a small, kind act that I can do today?" or "What is a small act of respect that I can perform today?" This needs to be small and immediate. Even something very small, such as calling somebody just to say hello, or looking someone in the eye when the person is making a request of you instead of continuing to read a magazine. It does not really matter what the deed is, as long as it is small and real.

---

3 *Hilchot Teshuvah*, chapter 1

Identify specific middot. Various deeds stem from the same middot, so identifying these middot is a core step. Hashem will not simply remove a negative middah. There has to be an awakening from below in order to draw down an awakening from Above, but Hashem does far more than we do. If you open yourself a little bit, Hashem will expand this opening far beyond what you can possibly imagine.

Another method of identifying your middot involves working from the inside out. We will discuss this in detail later in this text. Identifying your middot doesn't only mean identifying your negative ones, but also your positive traits. Any middah can be used positively or negatively. *Chessed* can be negatively manifested through manipulation, whereby you give to the other person because you believe that they either could be or should be changed, when they do not want to or cannot change. With *kavod*, there is the positive inner feeling that you get when you sacrifice something for the good, such as forfeiting potential profit for the sake of honesty. One of the highest levels of the soul is called *kavod*.

Talk to Hashem every day and ask for clarity. Ask Him for the ability to draw closer to Him. Say to Hashem, "I have been dealing with this issue for 20, 30 years. Hashem, today please be with me so that I can understand what is happening in order for me to draw closer to You. Please present me with the clarity that I need."

Compensation. You will need to make financial, physical or material compensation to the person if you harmed her in this way. As we have mentioned, this must be done through consultation with a Rav. You must not give up because you think that it is too overwhelming or too expensive.

Being Forgiven and Forgiving

If someone else was affected by your misdeed, it is necessary to ask that person for forgiveness. What is the easiest way to go about actually making this happen? If you try to ask her for forgiveness and it doesn't seem to be working, because you hurt her really deeply or in a way that makes it really difficult for her to forgive you, you have to realize that in the same way that Teshuvah is a process, forgiveness is a process. You therefore need to commit yourself to the process of making the other person recognize that you regret your choices and that you really want to do everything possible to change things.

This may involve you speaking to her several times. It may also involve you enlisting the aid of her friends (not your friends) to act as an intermediary on your behalf. Be prepared to make sincere efforts on your own part in addition to the interventions of others. When big issues are involved, this is completely reasonable.

If after you have made sincere efforts, the person is still unwilling to forgive you, then you have to be prepared to let go of it because you cannot live her life. At this stage, the one left dealing with the burden of self-definition is the other person. The exception to this rule is a parent or someone who taught you the majority of your Torah. In that case, no matter how many times you need to approach him or her, or reopen the case, you must stay in the picture until you gain forgiveness.

Forgiving your parents or a mentor. This is especially difficult, and even more difficult if what you did wrong was a direct result of the things they did. If this was the case, you still need to forgive them.

When it comes to forgiving your parents for damage they may have caused you, use Avraham Avinu as your model. Avraham's father, Terach, was by any measure a terrible parent. He turned his own son over to the authorities to be killed for the "crime" of believing in one G-d, yet Hashem deliberately chose him as Avraham's father rather than one of the tzaddikim of the time. However, in order for Avram to become Avraham, he needed to break idols. He needed that challenge for his own development. He needed to say, "This isn't who I am, I am someone else." It was *hashgachah* (Divine providence) that put Avram in that situation.

Similarly, it was hashgachah that made you the child of your parents, because from Hashem's perspective, they were the people who could bring out your maximum potential for growth in the way that nobody else in the world could. Therefore, you need to realize that their actions were all part of Hashem's plan for you. It is thus possible for you to say at this point that you understand why you shouldn't be angry, but why should you give kavod to a person who did all these things to you?'

At this point, you also need to realize that the reason behind respecting parents is twofold: first, there are three partners in the creation of a child, the third party being Hashem. The fact that there are three partners tells you that who you are is a direct inheritance from your parents. Biologically you are their offspring. There is no alternative. From this angle, the more you value your own life, the more you should value your parents for making you who you are.

You could of course say that you didn't ask to be born and your parents didn't make a conscious decision to make you who you are. This is true, but the error in thinking along these lines is you think that gratitude toward someone requires that the other person consciously wanted to benefit you. On the contrary. As long as someone benefited you, regardless of whether he and/or she did so consciously or unconsciously, *you owe them a debt of gratitude – and in the case of parents you need to be grateful to them just because you are here and they made you.*

When trying to forgive parents emotionally, you need to ask yourself honestly where your choices are taking you. For Avraham, this process had to do with his determining who he was regarding his relationship with G-d. Figuring that out had to begin with his figuring out who he was not. In figuring out who you are on a human level and on an emotional level, you have to acknowledge that you could have learned from your parents who you are and who you do not want to be emotionally.

Insufficient teshuvah. There is also a concept such as doing Teshuvah for insufficient Teshuvah. This happens when you did Teshuvah for something in the past, not because you saw it as damaging to yourself but because you didn't want to be held accountable for it by Hashem, or because you didn't appreciate the gravity of the damage for which you were repenting. It is also possible that you didn't appreciate the extent of Hashem's *rachamim* making it possible for you to change completely. *This year's Teshuvah could therefore be deeper and more authentic than last year's Teshuvah.*

SHIUR 2

Internal Goals of Teshuvah (Deeds)

Applying Middat Harachamim –
The 13 Attributes of Mercy[1]

Hashem "tolerates" us, let us tolerate others.

One of the central features of Selichot are the *middot harachamim*, which is why it is important to go over them. A deeper reason to go over them is that during Elul you have to focus on not simply the negative but also on the positive. You need to think about who you could be.

Once you have done your *cheshbon hanefesh* and have determined your basic middot, you need to realize that there is something even higher than you, something that lurks within you, which is the inherent part of you that is similar to Hashem. That part of you is the *tzelem Elokim*, and it is crucial to develop a relationship to it.

Tomer Devorah, the Ramak's classical work on drawing closer to Hashem, says that a person, by virtue of being created in God's image, should be striving to be similar to his or her Creator. *This is the deepest secret that we have, and likewise it is the most internal aspect of who we are.*

We tend to live lives, that at least some of the time, have nothing to do with the *tzelem*. We also tend to live lives in which our external and internal realities are often not connected. The secret of how to really learn this *tzelem* and make it part of you (as opposed to simply learning the middot, period, and how they relate to you), is from a passage in

---

1 See appendix. The Thirteen Attributes of Mercy

Michah (7:18–20): "Who is a force like You that carries sins of desire and that passes over sins of rebellion to the remnants of Your inheritance and doesn't hold on to anger forever because You love *chessed*." A short synopsis of the middot will be presented at the end of the book. We will focus on the most practical aspects of internalizing some of the middot here.

These thirteen attributes, which we will discuss shortly, operate as a continuum. As it says "You have given truth to Yaakov, kindness to Avraham as you swore to our ancestors in the earliest times."[2]

Mi Kel Kamocha – Who Is Like You Hashem?

"This is to teach you that Hashem is a humiliated King,"[3] i.e., Hashem tolerates insults. We cannot even let our imagination tell us the depths of this attribute because it is so enormous. Nothing is concealed from Hashem's *hashgachah*. He is fully aware of everything. There is no person in the world who is not sustained by His force at each second. This means that there isn't a single person, even one who is heavily steeped in real sin, who at each moment isn't being nurtured and sustained by His will. Even at that precise moment He gives each person the ability to move even though the person is using this power to commit a sin. Hashem tolerates this. There is no insult greater than to be given the gift of life and the ability to move, and then use this gift to go against the One Who has given it to you.

We need to realize that Hashem, Who is tolerating all of this, can do whatever He wishes to do. He would be able to prevent the person physically from being able to do what he is planning to do, and has indeed at times done so. Look at the case of Yerav'am ben Navat[4], who, after King Shlomo's death, took the kingdom for himself and moved from being a great tzaddik to an egocentric *rasha*. In order to prevent people from going to Yerushalayim where their spiritual focus should be, and in order that everyone should see his kingdom as the larger, more essential one, he built an alternative beit hamikdash. But this

2 *Micah 7:20;*
3 *Pirkei Heichalot, chapter 24;*
4 *Melachim 1, 13:4;*

wasn't a place cantered on the service of Hashem. He tried to ensure that people focus on him by giving power to his own false priests, his own *mizbe'ach* and his own imagery. In this way he brought *avodah zarah* back to the people.

At one point he was approaching the *mizbe'ach* in his beit hamikdash when Hashem paralyzed his hand so that he couldn't function anymore, exactly as it had been prophesied long before. Therefore if Hashem wanted to intervene to prevent these kinds of insults, He could, and it would be very reasonable for Him to do so. After all, it would make sense for Him to say, "If you want to sin against Me, then do so with your own strength and your own capacity, not with My strength." But Hashem does not do this.

We need only to look at our own lives to see how many times Hashem allowed us to do what was wrong, even though at the same time we had a great day and were wearing nice clothes. Tomer Devorah quoting the *Zohar* says that the angels praise Hashem mainly for this.

Adopting the middah of tolerating insults. If you want to be in touch with your G-dliness; the part of you that is like Hashem, the very first thing you have to do is adopt the middah of tolerating insults. That means that you have to let other people be themselves. You shouldn't form relationships based on mutuality. You should build relationships with people where your goal is to benefit them and to express/show goodness to them. You may be human enough to feel a bit of protest, saying, "If G-d punishes people for doing wrong, why shouldn't I do the same? I certainly know people who deserve it." You have to always remember that Hashem's thoughts are far beyond yours. His justice is always a manifestation of His inherent goodness.

About the concept of Hashem tolerating all of this, there is a deeper aspect to explore, namely, that during the process of returning to your higher self, you will notice that there are always two steps; one that you like and one that you dislike. The source of this is found in *Yechezkel*, where it says that the angels "go forth and they draw back."[5]

---

5 *Yechezkel* 1:14;

Two steps to Teshuvah: inspiration & return. When you do Teshuvah, there are also two stages involved. The first is inspiration, where you go forward and have a strong desire to change and to try to reach the levels of the tzaddikim. This is called *ratzon*, the inspiration that you feel deep inside you, even before you are challenged to find a way to express it in the real world. You need to see to what extent this inspiration is going to be real.

Stage two is called *shav* (return), which means that Hashem will definitely challenge you in order for you to be able to develop the potential that you acquired during the inspiration stage and actualize it through meeting the challenge. That is called *achar hadin* – after Hashem has already decreed that you should be challenged.

Here, you could ask which of the challenges that Hashem brings to people will move them the farthest? For instance, Rabbi Akiva 'needed' Romans, Hillel 'needed' poverty, and Avram 'needed' Terach. Now you need to ask what you need. The most universal of all challenges is this: Can I tolerate insult? Can I have a relationship that I will stay in and be there for that person regardless?

On the deepest of all levels, tolerating insult means that you have made it your life goal to give *kavod* to Hashem and not give *kavod* to yourself. Once you have passed that barrier, everything else comes readily. This is the hardest and therefore the first of all of the middot that put you in touch with the *tzelem Elokim* within you.

However, it is imperative that you never put yourself into a position in which it is likely that you will be the victim of insult, because you don't know how you will respond until after the fact. *There is a rule that you should never challenge yourself, as Hashem will decide when and under what circumstances you could bear the challenge.* An example would be, for instance, being sure that you know the "rules of the game" before entering new social situations with which you are unfamiliar.

The last few middot lead one into the other.

Creation of Destructive Forces

Nosei avon, which means that Hashem "carries" the destructive forces that you create when you sin, is similar to the previous middah, but is expanded and deepened.

Whenever a person sins he creates a destructive force. *Pirkei Avot* states that "a person who transgresses makes one accuser with each sin."[6] This accuser then stands before Hashem and says, "This person made me." Nothing could exist without Hashem's will, which means that this very destructive force that is standing before Hashem is a product of His will. Hashem could very easily choose not to sustain this destruction; He could tell the accuser to go to the one who created it and to draw its energy from him. At that point the destructive force would be aimed back at that person who created it, with three possible results. The destructive force could take the person's soul and cause his death. Or it could bring about the reality of his being cut off from Hashem, which is the punishment called *karet* (literally: cut-off;) *karet* could signify either an early death and dying without children, or losing the potential to experience his portion in the future life, or it could mean losing the relationship to the merit of the Jewish people; or, lastly, it could bring about punishment according to whatever sin the person did. You must always remember that only Hashem knows how long a specific person was meant to live. His lifespan is determined by Hashem's knowledge of how much time he needs to achieve the mission for which he was created. The same underlying concept has to do with Hashem's decision about how many children, if any, should be born to a specific family. You have no way of knowing whether someone else lived a short life because this is the amount of time he needed, or whether Hashem shortened his life because he had reached the point of no return due to his bad choices. You have no right to judge anyone else. You don't even

---

6 *Pirkei Avot* 4:13;

know with real clarity why your own life is contoured to fit the pattern that Hashem fashioned for your time in this world.

Logically, we might assume that the destructive force would be aimed at the person who created it. But that isn't what Hashem does. Instead, He tolerates this destructive force and the person who brought it into existence. He doesn't judge people immediately after their failures, nor does He punish them as soon as they begin to spiral downward (which is ultimately a *tikkun*).

For instance, a person can make so many bad choices that they are now the only options he considers. An example would be a person who claims falsely to be in need of tzedakah and habitually "embroiders" more reasons to support him; how likely is it that he will return a check that he pleaded for? Won't he just use the money? When he does, he has made his situation worse than it was before he was given the check. If this isn't just one aspect of the way he is living his life, he can reach a point in which each day only gives him more opportunities for self-destruction. In that case, Hashem taking him out of the world before his normal span of life would have ended, is a *chessed*. In the Next World, the good deeds that he did will have greater potential to define him when not outnumbered by the bad deeds he was denied the possibility of doing. In this sense, his early death is a *tikkun*. If he comes to realize that he has been making bad choices when he is faced with death, then even in this world a *tikkun* has occurred.

There are three possible reasons for Hashem allowing this:

a) Even though the person created the destructive force, his story may not be over. He may do Teshuvah and his Teshuvah may end the harm done by this destructive force.

b) Hashem will judge the person and Hashem will determine what will happen to him – not only to punish him for his deeds but also in order to change him. Hashem is Just in that He allows a person to suffer in this world so that this suffering can atone for what he did or inspire him to move forward.

c) The person will have to face Gehennom and derive his *kapparah* (atonement) there, but he will still attain *kapparah*.

The story in the Torah that seems to best illustrate this is the story of Cain. Cain murdered Hevel and when Hashem confronted him by asking him where his brother was, he responded by saying, "What, am I my brother's keeper?"[7] Hashem then told him that he must either do Teshuvah or face his sin. Cain then asked Hashem: "Is my sin too great to tolerate?"[8] You can tolerate the entire world, but you can't tolerate my one sin? He was trying to say that Hashem could tolerate Cain if He chose to do so. However, in Cain's case this would not have been good for Cain or for the world in general. For that reason, instead of ignoring his sin, Hashem cursed him. This could have opened the doors of change for him, if he would have taken advantage of the challenges that he now faced.

In order to understand this fully, we need to first grasp what is meant by a destructive force. If we were asked to name a sin that "creates destruction," the sin that usually comes to mind is lashon hara. This is embarrassing in and of itself, especially if we keep coming back to this point as an example. When you speak lashon hara, you may think that nothing happened – no lightning struck you down. Often you don't see the effect of the lashon hara on your victim or on the listener, whose vision of reality was warped by your sharing your negativity with him. Hashem is "letting you get away with it" in the short run, in order to give you the chance to notice how damaging negativity is, and from that point, to do Teshuvah.

We are like a person who finds himself in Israel where the bus-drivers by law are not obligated to exchange a 200-shekel note. Imagine yourself stepping onto a bus with no other money except a 200-shekel note and the driver, seeing that you are Jewish, will scream at you but take your money anyway. If this happens repeatedly with the same driver, he will start wondering, "Why is this person not getting it?"

---

7 *Bereishit* 4:9;
8 *Bereishit* 4:13;

Like the bus driver in the example, the day comes when the question "How come he's not getting it?" is relevant, especially since the harm he does is real.

When you speak lashon hara, the person who is least affected most of the time is the victim. Granted, there are times when the things you say can be exceedingly destructive, like causing a shidduch to founder or, *chas v'shalom*, a marriage to be ruined. Often you may be speaking lashon hara to a person who doesn't really know the person of whom you are speaking well enough to care about your negative judgments and unkind words. But even if your lashon hara doesn't cause direct harm to the victim, you are still creating negative energy.

The negative energy you are creating within yourself begins with your motivation. If you have done your *cheshbon hanefesh*, you should be able to determine what this motivation is. It could be that you are strengthening your trait of *kavod* in the negative sense, or that of pride or jealousy. What you are doing to the other person, however, (your audience), is creating a negative perspective on life that could change everything for her. It could ruin her *bitachon* or positivity toward other people. You have made it harder for both her and you to see the holy image of the Creator in His creation.

That is the destructive energy that was formed by your speaking lashon hara, and it has to go somewhere. However, it won't necessarily go back to you, meaning that Hashem will not always decide that because you were the one to bring this negative energy into the world, you should be the one to receive the brunt of the damage in a way that is direct and immediate.

Tolerating Negativity

What can you do with or about your feelings? You have to learn to tolerate the negativity, not just the insults and the force of the wrongs your friends and relatives may have done to you. This is especially true when the effects of their evil still exist. You should put up with it because your real goal is to be patient enough to wait until your friend or relative comes to their *tikkun. You don't need to continually defend yourself and be in a position of reaction.* When you do react, they feel almost as though they are defending their lives and autonomy. Reacting in kind imprisons you because it keeps you attached to the destructive energy that someone else created.

> A juvenile example of this would be a fifteen-year-old whose mother shouts aggressively, "Wear your coat, it's cold out! Your father and I work very hard for our money and we got you that expensive coat you wanted, not the one *we* would have chosen . . . so wear it!'. The fifteen-year-old responds by saying confrontationally, "It's not so cold out. If *you're* cold, *you* wear a coat," and then walks out into the snow.
>
> The adult version would be if your husband or child or boss says something that you don't like, and you find yourself getting into the mindset of "I will not be victimized," and you angrily respond to them on their terms.

This is called being reactive. In order to avoid being reactive, you need to ask yourself, "Who do I want to be?" Once you have a strong sense of who you want to be, you will want to defend that ideal. Therefore, when you are interacting with someone, you will be able to tell yourself that you do not want to lose your identity to them. By keeping this in mind, you will be able to prevent yourself from becoming someone you don't want to be. Remind yourself that you want to be the one to determine your identity, and you don't want to hand that control over to someone else.

In difficult situations, it can help to remember your *cheshbon hanefesh* and recall your strongest positive trait. You then need to think of actual instances when you used these strengths to their greatest advantage and how you felt about yourself when you succeeded. Use this memory to hold onto your goal of who and where you want to be in life and to avoid relinquishing your identity to others. This visualization should help to make it more real on an emotional level.

When a neighbor continually insults or disturbs you, remind yourself not to react to her on the same level. If your neighbor makes a lot of noise late at night, don't stay up late another night in order to pay her back. Then ask yourself if by not speaking to the neighbor directly about the problem, you are actually harming her. If what the other person is doing is wrong according to Halachah then you should get the matter out on the table for her sake. We know at some stage Hashem will punish that person because He wants her to change, and although you are obviously not going to punish her, you should at least make her aware of what she is doing. It is good to call the person early on in Elul and to say to her, for instance, "I know that in the past I said or implied that it was OK, but both you and I know that it is not. We need to talk about it."

Of course, it is important to remember that you do not need to be everybody's best friend. Quite the opposite in fact. You can and should be selective about who you allow into your inner circle. Not everyone belongs in your inner circle. There are three mitzvot of *ahavat Yisrael*, namely, speaking well of fellow Jews, respecting others and caring about their material needs.

You also do not need to place yourself within the range of another person's attacks or influence. But if Hashem placed you there by making that person a parent or sibling, you have to be strong and not let whatever they say feel like a dagger. Strengthen yourself emotionally so you can remain detached from the negative things they are saying.

You need to be able to tell yourself, "OK, this is Barbara and she is who she is for whatever reason. This has nothing to do with me." This means not allowing yourself to be defined by that person. The fact that the other person called you stupid or ugly doesn't make you stupid or ugly. Rather, you must turn this around and see those comments as a reflection of her own pain and insecurity, and that has nothing whatsoever to do with you.

Furthermore, ideally, once you decide not to be reactive and not to be afraid of this, then you have already changed. This doesn't mean that

you should pretend that the interaction didn't happen, but rather to interact with that person according to the three levels of *ahavat Yisrael*, in the same way that you are obligated to do with any other Jew. If your relationship isn't such that you need to maintain it, like someone who is neither related to you nor in the same workplace, then there is no need for you to select her as the person you will call on Erev Yom Kippur in order to clear the air. You do not need to go beyond the boundaries of your obligation to her.

Oveir al Pesha

This involves taking the same progression further. Hashem does not forgive us through a *shaliach*, even though our punishments often come through one. When a person trips going down the stairs and breaks his ankle, gravity and velocity were the *shaliach*, but forgiveness comes directly from Hashem. As it says: "*Ki im'cha ha'selicha.*"[9] This means that Hashem Himself is involved in the process of washing away the damage that the sin causes. We previously said that sin causes damage to the person who does it. This damage can be washed away, as it says: "Hashem washes away the filth of the daughters of Zion."[10] Hashem doesn't passively forgive; He actually sends the means of forgiveness and makes it happen. It is not a passive process, but an active one on His part.

On a human level, this means that ideally a person shouldn't say "*I* should fix what somebody else broke?! She created this negative situation; she ruined the relationship. Now *I* should fix it? *She* should fix it! If she made her bed, let her lie on it!" You need to proactively make it possible for the situation to improve in order for the restoration to happen. Don't wait for things to happen. You can take the initiative to repair, and you will have the merit of *tikkun olam*.

Make it easy for the other person to change. The first and most elementary step in this process is to make it easy for the other person to change by not embarrassing or belittling her in any way. When you don't embarrass or belittle but show that you believe in her, you are acting out the role that Hashem plays when He is involved in the role of forgiveness.

---

9 *Tehillim 130:4;*
10 *Yesha'yahu 4:4*

Forgiveness in Close and Family Relationships

Dealing with painful relationships is a million times harder when they involve your close family. It can be very embarrassing to pick up the phone when you haven't spoken to someone in five years, especially when you still believe that you are right in regard to whatever the quarrel was about. You need to ask yourself to what extent you are invested in the destructive energy that this harm is creating. What's in it for you emotionally to hold on to the status quo? You need to say, "I will be the one to fix this, even though I was not the one to break it." This is obviously not an easy task. But the more you believe in your desire to be the person you truly believe you could be, the less important it is to you whether the other person thinks she won the game or not.

The prophet says: *"Mib'sarcha al tit'aleim,"*[11] which means "Don't conceal yourself from your flesh and blood." We find that Avraham was willing to risk his life for his nephew, Lot, who had betrayed him. If there is someone whom Hashem put into our relationship circle through Providence, it is not right under almost any circumstance to let the relationship die, because it is providential that you are this person's flesh and blood.

If the person is not a relative, there is another consideration. The halachic definition of *sin'at chinam* (baseless hatred) isn't that you are yelling at someone, hitting someone or causing them financial harm but that you cut yourself off from them. Nevertheless, you are allowed to be self-protective. So, if someone physically threatens you, place yourself out of her range physically. If that person is an emotional threat to you, ideally you should reach a place where that cannot be construed as an issue.

In the interim, you don't need to make yourself emotionally accessible to that person, and therefore vulnerable to her. It's a real tightrope! You could have a detached relationship. If she is spiritually threatening to you, if she is a bad influence on you, then you need to distance yourself from her spiritually to protect yourself. That is allowed.

---

11 *Yesha'yahu* 58:7;

Sometimes the reason you distance yourself isn't emotional. There are technical realities that push people apart. In a case where the person is no longer in your life because you have switched jobs or moved, you can comfort yourself with the recognition that most people do not continue a relationship when the other person has moved, even if they were formerly good friends.

> I remember that when I lived in Giv'at Shaul, I was quite close to the women in the community, but now I have only one close friend from those days with whom I am still in contact. Even though we are no longer in touch, there are only positive feelings there.

The rules of *sin'at chinam* apply where it is normal to maintain a relationship, but you have decided that you just don't want to have anything to do with that person at all. You do not need to seek the person out, but you do need to be honest with yourself about what the situation actually is. Have you decided to cut her out of your life? If you have, you need to work through these feelings until you reach a place where you genuinely wish her well and you genuinely want to give her *kavod*. That's all you have to do; you don't need to reform your relationship. As stated before, not everyone belongs in your inner circle, but every Jew is part of you, and cutting off any part can't do you any good.

If the other person wants to distance herself from you, but you want to repair the relationship, you must accept that she is the one who can decide who is in her inner circle. All you can do is try to comply with all of the above to the best of your ability; the reality is that there are times when you need to accept that not everybody is obligated to be your best friend. You could therefore be required to respect her need for a certain amount of distance.

In a situation where it is a relative who has constructed an artificial distance, meaning that she does not relate to you in a way that is normal for the type of relationship it is, you should try to discover the source of her negative feelings and then do your best to resolve the problem. You can ask her directly what she is feeling and thinking, and whether there is anything you can do to improve the situation. If she is frum, an especially good time to do this would be during Elul and before Rosh Hashanah. If she is not interested, then it is possible that she just wants her space.

In a case where you haven't been on speaking terms with a close family member, a parent or sibling, for years, you may want to try recruiting someone whom that person likes to intercede on your behalf. You would therefore need to find someone who would be able to talk to their heart. This can be embarrassing for you, especially if it is someone that she likes, because it will require you to approach that someone very humbly and take up some of his/her time to share your feelings.

There may be times when you find yourself reacting negatively to someone else's decline in levels of Torah observance, such as *tznius*, for instance. You need to look within yourself and question whether this could be a result of feelings of disappointment with her, or where you identify with her too much so that you feel that when she is not dressed appropriately, it is in some way devaluing you. If this is the case, then the issue isn't really between you and her, but with yourself. Therefore, you need to develop yourself through your *cheshbon hanefesh* to the point where you don't need someone else to validate you through her deeds. You need to go back to the beginning stage where there was no judgment and work onward from there.

Hashem treats us the way we should treat a relative. This idea is found in many places in Torah, and especially in *Shir Hashirim*, where we are called Hashem's lover or sister. In the case of a relative, her suffering is your suffering. Your relationship is very different from that which you have with other people. *Yesha'yahu* says that "whenever we suffer, Hashem has pain."[12]

---

12 Yesha'yahu 63:9;

Relationship With Klal Yisrael

A person should ideally feel that same relationship with a relative and realize that the whole of Klal Yisrael should also be regarded this way, as we are all meant to be one unified soul. Feeling one with another person doesn't only mean feeling their pain, it also means identifying with what they are doing. You should want to feel part of Klal Yisrael and to experience a forward movement to the point that joining into a collective effort, such as *tefillah,* is done willingly. You should do it because you feel that you need to be there for them because they are all like relatives. This principle of seeing others as part of yourself, is crucial and is the key to many other concepts.

SHIUR 3

Internal Goals of Teshuvah (Middot)

The source for this section is a *Ma'amar* from Rebbe Nachman's *Likutei Moharan* I, Torah 14, entitled *Tik'u b'chodesh shofar*. (There is an English version available that was translated by Rabbi Chaim Kramer.) This particular *ma'amar* focuses on the topic of what happens when you blow the *shofar*[1].

Rebbe Nachman's mission statement is that our primary intention when we hear the *shofar*, as well as when we continue our lives after Rosh Hashanah, is to want to draw down shalom into the world. By using the word *peace*, he is referring to peace within ourselves, peace within our families, within Jewish communities, and within the greater world.

Dedicating Ourselves to the Honor of Heaven

People have searched for peace since the beginning of time. It remains elusive. Peace can't be imposed artificially. Outside intervention at best can prevent war (and even that is a dubious premise). For real peace to be sustained, there has to be a goal that goes beyond individual needs. The alternative is people setting their own goals which in all likelihood will clash with the path that others have chosen. The only way that there will ever be peace in all the above aspects is if we dedicate ourselves to *k'vod Shamayim*. His reasoning is that lack of direction leads to each person going his own way. When you aren't competing with others but directing your energies toward serving Hashem, you will feel the kind of peace that never lets you fall into the trap of feeling separate from

---

1 *Tehillim 81:4; "Blow a shofar on the New Moon, on the day it is hidden; for the day of our feast..."*

and threatened by, other people. Therefore, what we share with every blade of grass and certainly with every attribute in our characters, as well as with every Jew and every human being, is that within us, on the deepest level, our root has an awareness of Hashem. This awareness applies even to inanimate things. The Rebbe goes on to explain that we have to elevate the *kavod* of Hashem from its very root. This root of all things is that consciously or, not everything contains a certain element of *yir'at Hashem*.

+ *"Torat chessed"* is a phrase that comes from *"Eishet Chayil"*?[2]: The only way that we could ever elevate Hashem's glory is through *Torat chessed* – the Torah that is realized through *chessed*.

+ Learning in order to teach is the mainstay of Hashem's *kavod*, but it refers not only to academic teaching and learning. *Chazal* teach us that true *chessed* comes about when we learn and our intent is to teach.

+ The *Zohar* tells us that "at the time when the nations (goyim) come and see the light of Hashem, at that moment the *kavod* of Hashem departs from its place of concealment and is glorified in the world. This applies to the upper world and to the lower world."[3]

The 'Upper World' and the 'Lower World' (Our World)

It is possible to live in the world and to seek kavod shamayaim without burying your head in the ground. The concept of an upper world refers to the fact that Hashem is unknowable and infinite. He then translates His presence to this world (our world) through a series of contractions. These are compared to veins that bring lifeblood to all the different limbs and organs of the body. If, G-d forbid, there is a blockage that prevents the flow of blood, the limb that is affected does not receive blood and dies. Hashem never changes, so, if a person creates blockages, our ability to know Hashem and to have meaning in our lives in

---

2 *Mishlei* 31:26; 'She opens her mouth with wisdom, and a lesson [Torah] of kindness is on her tongue."
3 *Zohar Yitro, 69a;*

order to live lives that are good and noble, is then killed, in a sense. By creating blockages to good, we are opening ourselves up to the influence of external forces and creating the negative challenges that we call evil. This is what is meant in the book of the prophet *Malachi* by Hashem's words "I Myself don't change." [4]

This leads to us living in a world where, although Hashem has not changed, we can bear witness to all the terrible things that we read in the paper. The fact that these occurrences could happen indicates a certain kind of spiritual death. Therefore, the main *tikkun* suggested by the *Zohar* is for us to bring down Hashem's light into the world in a way that is evident and real in us, and is so powerful that it even reaches the non-Jewish world.

We might view this as being strange because we do not generally have a goal of inspiring converts. But the rule is that "the stronger the pitch, the further the ball goes." The stronger our *kavod* is, the more likely it is that even someone who is very distant from us is affected by us. This could even be a non-Jew on the other side of the world.

The *Zohar* continues: "When Yitro said, 'Now I know that Hashem is greater than all other gods,' at that moment Hashem's *kavod* flowed down to the world."

This is what we want, of course. The idea here is that if you take people who are outside the realm of *kedushah* (holiness) and you draw them close by your example, the result is that both they and the world will be changed. This is what *kabbalat 'ol malchut Shamayim* means, namely, that you are accepting upon yourself to lead that kind of life. The Rebbe says that the effect is evident when you see the presence of *geirim* (converts) and ba'alei teshuva, of whom we are seeing more and more in our times. This indicates that the cumulative acts of *Torat chessed* (from throughout the generations up to and including ours, where the internal Torah is manifested externally in their lives) are now affecting the world to the extent that we are now seeing the entry (into our ranks) of *geirim* and ba'alei Teshuvah as never before.

---

4 *Malachi* 3:6;

Bringing Down Hashem's *Kavod* by Example

"But the kavod of Hashem is in exile and the main kavod is among the goyim themselves, and the Jews are lowered and humiliated" (Likutei Moharan).

When people in the world say, "Wow, I want to be like that person," the next sentence usually isn't "I wish I was more like the Jews." However, when the Mashiach comes, Hashem's *kavod* is going to be revealed in the midst of this darkness. The result will be that everyone will want to serve Hashem like people who are working toward achieving the same goal, shoulder to shoulder. Therefore, the first answer to the question of how we bring down Hashem's *kavod* is "By Example." This means that the litmus test for whether you are truly living a life *lichvod yir'at Shamayim* or not is whether your deeds are real enough to affect people.

K'vod Hashem Through Your Deeds

"The only way that we can have this kavod of Hashem flow to other people through your deeds is through the Torah itself" (ibid.).

People have the mistaken idea that we might somehow bring *kavod* of Hashem by fluently speaking the language of the place we live in, or by dressing well or having skills that are viewed by society as being significant. However, this is a tragic mistake as it doesn't bring *kavod* of Hashem. Rather, it creates anti-Semitism because people feel as though we are stealing their roles. The proof is found in *Mishlei*, where it says: "Your wellsprings have to break forth and spread outwards."[5] The emphasis here is on *Your* wellsprings, because the Torah is compared to water. This means that you have to water them from the outside, as other people do not have this within them. People who have no connection to Hashem are on the other end of the deadened limb.

"*There is no kavod except Torah.*"[6] Rebbe Nachman then quotes a passuk from *Yirmiyahu* in which the prophet says, "Can you take

---

5 *Mishlei 5:16;*
6 *Pirkei Avot, 6:3;*

that which is high honor from that which is cheap?"[7] He continues: "so *Chazal* say that the way that you take something honorable from that which is cheapened is when your draw people to *avodat Hashem*, because every person is called a source of Divine *Kavod*." Every person has a way in which they too can bring *k'vod Shamayim* into revelation through their lives.

Finding the Mitzvah That Resonates With You Personally

"*The Torah has 600,000 letters*"[8] (ibid.). There is actually a specific way to calculate this, for if you just count each letter as is, you will see that this number isn't reached. However, when you take into consideration that some of the individual letters are actually comprised of several letters, such as the aleph, which consists of a vav and two yuds, we are able to reach the correct number that represent the number of souls of the Jewish people. Although there were 600,000 Jews who came out of Mitzrayim, today there are at least 14 million Jews in the world, so we need to consider what this means, namely, that the number 600,000 represents our root souls.

All our individual souls are therefore like branches of a root soul, and each soul is associated with a specific letter in the Torah. This is an aspect of the Torah that resonates with you sometimes when you feel instinctively a certain kind of deep connection to someone whom you barely know. Your soul and that soul may have a common root. All the roots take you back to the Torah, the Tree of Life. Therefore, every Jew, both men and women, has some aspect of Torah that resonates with them internally.

---

7 *Yirmiyahu* 15:19;
8 Based on *Shaar HaGilgulim, Rav Chaim Vital*, in the name of the *Ariza"l*;

An example of this is what one man did whose wife was killed in the attack on the Number 2 bus in Jerusalem. The mitzvah that resonated with this man and his wife had always been the mitzvah of *hachnasat orchim* – feeding people. This couple would host between fifty to one hundred yeshiva bachurim for Shabbos meals every week – mainly from Mir but also from Brisk. They had a tiny apartment that could perhaps comfortably fit six people at the table, so they would seat people on the couch and on the floor and on the stairs. They did not have much money, and yet one of the main features of these meals was the enormous chulent pot that was as big as a person. People flocked to them because the feeling of warmth and welcome was unparalleled. These people found their mitzvah. When this man was speaking in memory of his wife, he said that one of his first considerations now was: What's going to be with Shabbos?

This reflects the way in which people need to find the mitzvah that resonates most with them. That is their portion in Torah. Once they find it and give it expression in the world, it is going to affect the world, especially those who share that root. The idea is that because the Torah is a single thing, it affects everybody.

"*The souls of Israel arose in Hashem's mind before anything else.*"[9] When you bring Torah into the world "this is the *zivug* of the soul." You are connecting your soul and the soul of everyone else with its Source. In the same way that the actual *zivug* between the soul of a man and a woman is the union between the one who gives forth and the one who receives, when you find the Torah that is your Torah, you attach it to yourself and it is called *zivug*.

"*The brilliance and the dazzling ruchniut force is the result of the zivug, the spiritual union. And through the brilliance of this zivug, the souls of the gerei tzedek come into being*".[10]

This *zivug* then bears children who would be the Ba'alei Teshuvah and

---

9 *Bereishit Rabah 1;*
10 *Zohar, Shelach pg. 168;*

geirim. These souls are transformed from being ordinary citizens of the world, into *gerei tzedek*, meaning that something resonates within them. This is the inherent potential Jewishness with which they were created.

Bringing Light Through Deeds Resonates With Others

"Even the rebellious who are anti-Torah are illuminated through this. Even that [rebellious] soul still has a relationship with the Ultimate Root of Hashem Himself from which it stemmed" (ibid.).

When you bring some light, that person's soul resonates and he relates what he is feeling to his Root, either consciously or subconsciously.

An example of this occurred when the Israeli soccer team was in Ukraine to play a major game against the Ukrainian team. The game was played in one of the main stadiums and children climbed over the fence and sat on the edge of the turf because they couldn't afford to buy tickets. In the middle of the game, torrential rain began to fall. One of the members of the Israeli team saw a little boy who looked like he was around nine years old sitting on the turf and shivering. So he took off his own jacket and gave it to the child. Immediately, the other members of the Israeli team did the same. In the meantime, the Ukrainian team was standing there holding onto their jackets. The Ukrainian news service took a picture of this with all the Israeli team members standing in the rain without jackets while these poor children were wearing oversized sports jackets. This was then picked up by the international media and broadcast around Europe.

Something in that deed, which these players may or may not have known, comes from the Torah, and resonated within them, and then with everyone, which is why observers felt a need to publicize it.

Therefore if you want to influence those who are unaffiliated with Torah, the best way to do it is to identify with them and then externally express a concept of Torah that resonates within you. This in turn will trigger a reaction within the souls of others. For this reason, Rav Aaron

Leib Steinman says that in regard to the current political situation in Israel, the best thing for Jews to do is to learn more, because this is what will resonate an awakening within the souls of other Israelis.

"How can it be that you sometimes find that talmidei chachamim don't have children who are talmidei chachamim?"[11]

In today's world it isn't unusual to find people who live good lives but don't always evn succeed in influencing their families, let alone the world. You have to look at things as they are; there are so many reasons that children leave the path of Torah in today's world. Not every child is fortunate enough to attend a school that really is there for him; and in truth, no school can possibly address the needs of each child's individual personality and needs. Not every child is fortunate enough to come from a family that is warm and loving. Not every child is fortunate enough to have parents who are at peace with each other, and give each other the emotional support that makes their message credible. Not every family is one in which structure is provided along with love. Not evey child has the inner fortitude to resist the messages that the geater society projects, they are affected by the the rigid libralism that relegates morality to a narrow corner barely to be tolerated, and they are affected by the media. There are so many factors to consider that you may find yourself asking, "How come the vast majority of kids stay on track?" The worst mistake of all, the Gemarah tells us, is one that many parents manage to avoid. The Gemarah says, that the reason for the exile (which is the source of all of the evils we just mentioned) is that they didn't say Birkas HaTorah. This isn't just literal, there are many different levels of saying Birkat HaTorah.

"Everyone, especially a talmid chacham who learns or puts Torah into practice, needs to relate it to the Root of all souls; one has to relate it to Hashem and recognize that this is what resonates in his soul. This is what a brachah does."

The word *baruch* means "the source of all blessing." When we say, "You are the Source of all blessing," we have to be careful to ensure that we

---

11 *Talmud Bavli, Nedarim 81a;*

do not see the Torah as being separate from Hashem. Therefore, as a person is learning and reflecting on all the different arguments and explanations, the goal isn't simply to understand the *sugya* but to know that through this, he wants to reveal Hashem. If that is lacking, the light he could shed remains where it was. However, if he really thinks that, the effect is the opposite.

"If a person is learning with that intent, the light will be transferred to the person's child and it will affect the child, because it is so bright and so brilliant."

This is why you sometimes find rabbinical dynasties.

"It affects our children, because our souls are asleep in exile. The soul doesn't have its own luminosity unless somebody awakens it by saying or doing something that resonates."

Therefore, it is common to find with people who go "off the derech" that they will say that the frum community are living for their own *kavod* and to simply make a good impression. They will say this because they feel internally that this [Torah] is not resonating on some level. The reason that it is not resonating is because their souls are asleep and what they are receiving isn't enough to awaken them.

"The only way that you will find your cheilek (portion) in Torah is through humility. As Chazal say, 'The Torah is given as a gift in the desert to someone who makes himself like a desert."[12]

Such a person makes himself ownerless to the extent that what he has, he gives away freely. He has no desire for ownership, so to him, letting go of possessions is not emotionally difficult, since he never felt that they belong to him.

"In order to do this [find your cheilek], you need to be focused on four different things. First, to give expression to your own smallness." The Orchot Tzaddikim explains, "The more you allow yourself to see

---

Hashem's greatness, the more you will feel your own smallness."[13] This doesn't mean viewing yourself as bad, unsuccessful or a less valuable person, but that you are awed by Hashem's *gadlus* to the point that you say, 'What am I?'

> How can someone like me, really think about Hashem? I live in the real world!

Hashem's *Seichel* and His *Chochmah*

There are two ways to open yourself to Hashem's *gadlus*: by seeing His a) – *chochmah*/wisdom; and b) – *seichel*/intelligence.

Be 'wowed' by the world. The concept of wisdom can be understood through the passuk: "How great are Your deeds Hashem, You made them all with *chochmah*."[14] When you are walking outside and see roses, you say "Aha! Hashem, You created red! No one could even imagine [on his own] what that is, and Hashem created color for us as a gift." You can apply this to anything. The concept is the same as if you were to buy your seven-year-old the dream gift of a miniature car that he could drive himself. The response that the parent expects from the child then is for him to be very appreciative and excited, and not simply brush it off. So too, Hashem created this incredible intricacy and beauty in order to give us a way in which to connect to Him and to feel His love for us.

Be Open to Seeing Hashem's Hand in Your Day-to-Day Life

Seeing Hashem's *seichel* means recognizing His *hashgachah*. The way you experience Hashem's Hand is different from the way anyone else who ever lived did. Therefore, reviewing all of the *hashgachah* in your life helps you to gain a sense of Hashem's individuation.

---

13 *Orchot Tzaddikim – The Ways of the Tzaddikim*. The Second Gate. the Gate of Humility;
14 *Tehillim* 104:24;

The more you see Hashem's *chochmah* and *seichel*, the more you are in a place where you can say, "But I am small. Who am I to receive this?"[15] – in the same way that a child would be overwhelmed by receiving a miniature car.

The Four Dimensions of Feeling Small:

1) *Feeling small in relation to people who are truly great.*

That means being in absolute submission to the *Gedolei Torah* who are more learned than you because they bear Hashem's will and His message.

An illustration of this is the case of an Israeli student of mine who had an experience with a Rav who used bad judgment in dealing with her. It wasn't evil, just bad judgment, and the end result was that she was quite seriously humiliated. She said that it was now hard for her to accept rabbinical authority. I therefore told her that she had no choice, because they are her ladder to Hashem. I know people who have had negative experiences with doctors. They may have been dealt with abruptly, not given the full picture of the treatment options available, or worse still, treated as though they don't own their own bodies. Even if you are one of those people, performing your own appendectomy is probably not a choice you would consider.

The more you are aware of your own limitations, the readier you will be to bend your head down and accept their words.

2) *Lowering yourself before people who are on your level.*

This means looking at them for their Torah, because their Torah is what will resonate with you. You do not have the resources within yourself to recognize every aspect of Torah. You therefore need other people

---

15 *Bereshit* 32:11; *Ya'akov, the Patriarch: "I am unworthy of the least of the mercies and of all the truth, which You have shown to Your servant."*

whom you can look at to see their light. You need to be able to put your head down before it.

3) *Lowering yourself to people who are definitely less than you.*

Rav Shlomo Zalman Auerbach was an artist at this. When he first took up the position of Rosh Yeshivah of Kol Torah, he lived in the Shaarei Chessed neighbourhood of Jerusalem and refused to take a taxi or be driven to Bayit Vegan; he insisted in going by bus. He said, "Everyone goes by bus, the proof being that the buses are crowded." He did this until his age forced him to look for other options. Even then he would not allow the yeshivah to provide him with a driver. He did, however, agree to take a taxi. Every time he met a new cab driver, he would ask him friendly questions such as his name and where he was from.

Rav Shlomo Zalman was blessed with a phenomenal memory, so the next time he encountered the same diver, he would address him by name and ask him how things were in his area. Four different drivers attended his funeral, each one of whom was absolutely positive that he had been the Rav's private driver, because the Rav knew him so well.

One particular driver reflected out loud on how he enjoyed Eastern Sephardic music. Most Ashkenazim do not enjoy it, but he would play it when Rav Shlomo Zalman was riding with him. One day the Rav said, "I've heard your music, and you know what? I would like you to hear my music too." He then gave him a cassette of Mordechai ben David. He could just as easily have asked the driver to turn off the Mizrachi music, but he didn't. Instead he let that be a focus of sharing, as if to say "You like inspirational music and so do I, we are just touched by different approaches to it."

A different driver was a chain-smoker. Rav Auerbach didn't smoke even back when people didn't know that it was unhealthy. So the driver asked Rabbi Auerbach if he would mind him smoking. Now, people who do not smoke are not generally fond of the smell of cigarette smoke. Yet Rav Auerbach said, "Of course I want you to smoke. I enjoy seeing people doing the things they enjoy."

He treated these people, who were less than he, as people from whom he could learn and enjoy. However he never forgot that he was the general and they were the soldiers, and this is what is meant by "more than and less than." If he did not continually bear this in mind he would have risked leading people to chaos instead of providing a positive example.

4) *Learning to lower your head even before the smallest of the small.* This refers to people who are difficult, whose souls are torn apart or people with whom you wouldn't choose to be friendly.

> I once had a student who was brilliant, warm and charismatic. She suffered terribly as a child as a victim of abuse. As you might expect, her self-esteem was shattered. She responded to this by being extremely manipulative to "compensate" for how much she had been humiliated throughout her horrific childhood. This involved getting money from people through exerting emotional pressure on them for non-existent needs. She told many, many lies. But, because of her other qualities, there were three responses that people had toward her: some dropped her completely; some tried to help her by finding her a psychologist; and others chose to relate to her in terms of what is good. She had some hard-core friends who really knew the score with her, and had learned how to live with it.
>
> It happened that she was celebrating her birthday, so these friends organized a party for her. Two of the people in her life were Rabbi (*zt"l*) and (*tbl"c*) Rebbetzin Diskind from Baltimore, both beautiful people who lived in Har Nof. They used to invite her frequently for Shabbos. These were intelligent people who certainly knew what was going on, but pretended that they didn't. Her friends invited Rebbetzin Diskind to the party and she went. She later confided in someone, "I'm 85 years old. I have never in my life eaten in a restaurant, but what wouldn't I do for Evelyn (pseudonym)." Needless to say, the restaurant in question had the highest level of kashrut certification, Nevertheless Rebbetzin Diskind never ate out; that was the standard she had accepted upon herself for at least eight decades. Now she had to decide what to do. It was clear that if she either didn't come or didn't eat, the girl would have felt rejected, rationally or not. The Rebbetzin was able to put her head down before the smallest of the small.

5) *Learning to accept yourself, see your own inner kavod, and believe that you have something to contribute.*

This means recognizing that while you are small in comparison to Hashem, you are also committed to seeing your own *kavod*, the part of you that is eternal, valuable and in G-d's image, and to being able to bring it forth. The way you "learn" your mission in life, is by observing what choices Hashem has put in front of you, and what abilities He gave you. You can figure out what your hidden abilities are by thinking about what you are drawn to. These potentials are meant to be used. [16]

> Going back to the couple who were strong in *hachnasat orchim*, I personally am not drawn to that sort of thing. I like having guests, but I cannot imagine enjoying checking the amount of beans and barley that would be required for their chulent, never mind handling a pot that size. I don't have that kind of warmth of heart that would extend so far into feeding people who are hungry. However, there are things that do move me, such as reaching out to people intellectually. I like the *mekomot hakedoshim* and *tefillah*. Everyone needs to figure out what moves them. That is their place of *kavod*.

Hashem will sometimes tell us experientially that we guessed wrong. He will do this by putting us in life situations that will require us to discover a different part of who we are; at times you may find that your *nisayon* (challenge) doesn't necessarily resonate.

Hashem therefore informs us through the *nisayon* that Shabbos is His place of *kavod*. It is for this reason the Ariza"l[17] tells us that Shabbos is the place of greatest *gilui* in this world and that it is even greater than Yom Tov. He then explains that the highest part of Shabbos is in Mussaf during *chazarah* in the *Kedushah*, where we say, "Where is His place of glory?" then answer that the whole world is full of possibilities to manifest His *kavod*. That is the *ikkar* [main principle] of *kavod*.

---

16 See the Overview of the Vilna Gaon's commentary on Sefer Yonah for the concept that Hashem sends the soul to this world for tikkun olam (to rectify the world); and for tikkun atzmo (to rectify himself).

17 *Sha'ar Hakavanot* of Rabbi Chaim Vital in the name of the Ariza"l;

Look Inside, Then Look Outside... and Don't Forget to Enjoy the Trip

Essentially this means that you must first look within yourself to evaluate what it is that you are capable of, and then look at what the world is offering you as an opportunity, given the individual nature of your life. It doesn't matter whether you are enjoying your life! Don't feel guilty for doing what you were created to do when you spend your life doing what you can to bring Hashem's *kavod*. The consequence of this is that somewhere within you, you are using your *shoresh* (root) to draw down the *shoresh hashorashim* (Divine Root).

Avoid Self-Deception – See the Value in Others

The reason you need to first work on your relationship with people before you work on your relationship with yourself is that, like the rest of us, odds are that you can be very self-deceptive. This stems from the fact that you may not like yourself. You may first need to go through the steps of learning to see the value in others. The next step takes you into yourself and beyond. Giving Hashem *kavod* isn't about self-absorption. It is not about our achievements and our middot. It is about our will to draw Hashem into the world because of our own resonance and feelings of inner trembling before Him.

When we are instructed to give honor to those who have *yir'at Hashem*[18], it is Hashem's way of telling us that this is not just an instruction but a logical consequence. *Yir'ah* is therefore the state of resonance and inspiration, and *kavod* is the outward expression of this.

"As long as Hashem's kavod is in exile, everyone, to some extent, cheapens Hashem's Yir'ah."

This is because in *galut* we cannot see the whole picture; the resonance we would feel if we only felt Hashem's glory, is lacking. But, when you *metaken* (repair) it through taking whatever light there is into your own personal *galut* and bringing it outward, you bring *kavod* of Hashem to yourself. This makes self-acceptance a critical part of this process. You therefore need to begin by recognizing that you are in *galut* and accepting that this is your reality but still maintain the awareness that there is a place of *kavod* of Hashem within you.

---

18 *Tehillim* 15:4;

"Everybody has his own tikkun." Everyone has his own tools to use to rectify the *galut* and draw down Hashem's *kavod*.

"The ikkar is that when you are giving kavod to those who fear Hashem, it has to come from a full heart." It is crucial when bringing *kavod* of Hashem both into you and into others, that you allow the resonance to enter within you so that you can feel something. If you enter into the competitive mode, where you start feeling that "Well, what I do is also important," or into the threatened mode where you feel that "I cannot do anything," or into the reactive mode, and so on, you will find it more difficult. We need to realize, as is brought down in the *Gemarra*, that "of all things, that which is left to the heart more than anything is *yir'at Hashem*[19]. And it is within your own heart that *k'vod Hashem* exists."

So, even though prior to this we were emphasizing the importance of giving an outward expression of *yir'at Hashem*, we are now saying that its main place is within your own heart. When you have this kind of *yir'ah*, you are worthy of shalom. Therefore, the *ikkar* is to avoid that which is mentioned in *Yesha'yahu*, when the *Navi* discusses the people of his generation, saying, "with his [the generation's] mouth and lips, they give Me *kavod*, but they have removed their hearts far from Me."[20]

When You Break Down the Barriers, You Will See You Lack Nothing

As we have previously mentioned, shalom is when there are no *mechitzot* (barriers); where you can see Hashem's *hashgachah* in every occurrence in your life. This means in yourself as well as in others, including those who are above you and those who are below you because you see the commonality of the *yir'at Hashem* within them. The first way you feel this shalom is within yourself.

A person is often not at peace with himself, because he doesn't like himself and is not accepting of himself. However, if you accept that you are in *galut* while still maintaining an awareness of the *kavod* of Hashem within you, you don't have to pretend that you are perfect or

---

19 *Talmud Bavli, Kiddushin 32b;*
20 *Yesha'yahu 29:13;*

feel guilt-ridden about your mistakes. You are capable of being honest with where you are and the manner and extent to which you are capable of bringing forth Hashem's *kavod*. A certain degree of acceptance within yourself, according to the *Zohar*, means that *"when you have yir'at Hashem as your ikkar identity, then that is where there is sheleimut."* [21]

"There is nothing lacking for those who fear Hashem.[22]*"* This means that a person with *yir'at Hashem* never feels that he is lacking. Whatever personal challenges he has are opportunities for him to bring about *yir'at Hashem.* The external challenges presented to him come from the same awareness that extended to him the redness of the rose. Therefore, the first level of *yir'at Hashem* comes from within yourself, and then extends to the way in which it is manifested to others.

Based on all the above, we now have an idea of where our thoughts should be when we hear the *shofar,* namely, we should be hearing our inner *ratzon* to be accepting Hashem as a *Melech (King)*. Let yourself feel His *kavod,* because every soul trembles before it.

SUMMARY: *The Shofar should elicit our acceptance of Hashem as King and open your heart to k'vod Shamayim.*

The first step is to find the Torah that resonates within you and then to manifest it into the world, and that in turn will affect others because there is something that resonates within them as well. This includes secular Jews and even goyim. This is done through the four levels of humility: 1) first, before those who are greater than you; 2) then before those who are equal to you; 3) then smaller than you and then those who are even smaller; 4) and then to yourself. This will allow you to accept your own *galut* and to look for the place within you that can express *yir'at Hashem.* Doing this, leads to shalom within yourself and then shalom with the world.

---

21 *Zohar Yitro, 79a;*
22 *Tehillim 34:10;*

This should be your intent when listening to the *shofar* blowing. The test of whether you are truly acting from a place of *yir'ah* is to honestly ask yourself if you would still do this action even if no one was aware of it.

ASSIGNMENT: This week, at least, try to track all your encounters with people, from the greatest to the smallest, and then with yourself. Try to do this at the end of the day and say to yourself, "How can I bring *kavod* to each relationship?"

SHIUR 4

Tefillot of Rosh Hashanah and the Idea of Kabbalat Ohl Malchut Shamayim and Practical Applications

The mitzvah of Rosh Hashanah isn't mentioned as Yom Din in the Torah. In fact, it is not even hinted at anywhere that it is a day of judgment. It is, however, mentioned as a day of *shofar*-blowing. This tells us that the essential statement about what Rosh Hashanah is comes forth from our blowing the *shofar*.

We hear the 100 blasts over the course of the service and it is difficult to understand how to direct our thoughts in a specific sense. The clearest and most basic *kavanah* is that we want *k'vod Hashem* to come into the world.

The Three Sounds of the Shofar

Tefillah isn't enough. Unlike words, the voice has no demarcations. The sound of the *shofar* should take you to a place within yourself that doesn't have limitations or much definition. Nonetheless, each of these specific types of *kolot* (sounds) should help direct you toward a different train of thought.

The *Mishnah* tells us that the *shofar* cannot come from any animal whose horn would be called, "*keren*."[1] The word *keren* means "horn." It

---

1 *Mishnah Rosh Hashanah 3:2; see also Talmud Bavli, Bava Kamma 2b;* "Goring is only done by means of the horns." Going forth and hurting others is not acceptable behaviour. As such, the horn, a protruding appendage which alludes to going forth and goring, should not be used on *Rosh Hashanah*.

is used to describe something that goes forth from something else. The word *shofar* is related to the word *lehish'taper* – "to improve or beautify," and means the kind of horn that brings forth the inner will of the self to improve, *lehish'taper*. This idea can only be applied to something that already exists. For instance, it is not possible to renovate the living room unless there is a living room waiting to be improved.

Sometimes when you talk about self-improvement, you find yourself groping. You need to clarify how you want to be better, in what way and to what end. *Lehish'taper* therefore means to improve your contact with what is G-dly within in you, in order to make it possible for you to use this element to reach out toward Hashem.

When we are preparing for the *shofar* blasts, we say "*Min hameitzar*" (From the narrow straits I have called You ...)[2] seven times, which represent the seven times that the Jewish people surrounded the walls of Jericho. When they blew the *shofarot*, all the walls fell down. Similarly, our *kavanah* through reciting these verses seven times is that we should be able to bring down the walls around ourselves. There are no words to express this will.

The RaMaK (Rabbi Moshe Cordovero)[3] explains that "*the Ten Days of Teshuvah parallel the ten sefirot, the attributes that describe the way Hashem rules His world, and simultaneously describe the traits that we share in common with Him.*" The ten *sefirot* are expressed through each day of Teshuvah, meaning that on each day a different way of relating to Hashem becomes more accessible to us. When all these aspects are used appropriately, we are able to achieve what the kabbalists call "a whole building." This is a metaphor for all your traits being devoted to Hashem's *kavod*, and experiencing the resultant inner peace that can only be yours when you aren't at war with yourself. All we can do is connect with Him through the way in which He expresses His own story. We need to want to go back to each aspect of what Hashem is projecting Himself as being through the ten *sefirot*. By making use of

---

2 *Tehillim 118:5;*
3 One of the earliest kabbalists of Safed, (1522–1570), in his book *Tomer Devorah;*

this process, we are able to achieve full Teshuvah. Teshuvah means returning to the holiest and highest place.

The RaMaK then tells us that *hearing* means to really grasp the idea that the other person is trying to convey. Therefore, when we listen to the *shofar*, we want to hear the voice within ourselves that is calling to us to break down the barriers that are preventing us from knowing what we want and being able to reach that place. This voice below awakens a parallel voice from Above, because Hashem wants to hear us. His hearing us means that He penetrates us and really understands us to our core. Our hearing Him, through *binah*, means really understanding who you are, what the world is, and how Hashem's presence is the force from which everything comes. There is another trait. It is called *malchut*, which means kingship. You use *malchut* when you "hear" *binah* talk to you, and answer her "voice" by serving Hashem down here, practically, and with serious commitment.

How Do You Bring *Binah* into Your Heart When You Hear the *Shofar*?

When the *shofar* is blown, let yourself yearn. Hashem responds, so to speak, by saying, "I want them. I see what they are and what is inside them." He responds to your search by searching for you, using His *binah*. He can penetrate all of our layers and understand what is in our very core. This is why the brachah is "*lishmo'a kol shofar*."[4] Whenever we find the word *hearing* used, it is meant to convey this idea of penetrating until we really hear the One Who is speaking. When *binah* is translated into action you reach out toward the One Whose voice you hear. This reaching out is called *malchut*.

Binah is therefore called "the mother" because the mother gives birth to something, which in this case is *malchut*: our desire to submit to Him, and for Him to rule us.

Practically, this means that the basic concept to bear in mind when hearing the *shofar*, is to think, "I want to hear You Hashem, and I want

---

4 Literally 'to hear the voice of the shofar';

to do whatever I have to, to hear all of the time, at every minute." This is the voice of the *shofar* from below and this is what *malchut Shamayim* does.

As an aside, this intrinsic connection between *binah* and *malchut* is also why, even though a person is *yotzei* (has fulfilled the mitzvah) with lighting Shabbos candles if she has only one candle, the tradition is to light two candles. Although the main explanation that people are familiar with in connection with the candles is that of *shamor v'zachor*, these two words are also connected to *binah* and *malchut*. *Zachor*, stresses the importance of knowing who you are, where you are going and where you want to express light. *Shamor* is required in order to knock down the obstacles to achieving this goal.

Therefore, the voice itself, on the most basic level, is coming from inside you. This is the part of you that wants connection. This basic voice has three distinct voices. Each one of these voices awakens something specific. It is not just a variation on a similar theme.

a) *Tekiah*:

According to the SheLaH Hakadosh[5], this long voice parallels a simple desire to extend yourself. This desire is awakened when you experience Hashem's *chessed*. It says, "*Who is the true Chassid? The one who does chessed for his Creator.*"[6] However, Hashem doesn't need anything which means that our definition of *chessed* is erroneous. Here we are not talking about the act, but about the underlying *middah* that gives birth to the deed. The *middah* is wanting goodness, i.e. the desire to be good and to express goodness. This can be expressed through our relationships with other people, through the deeds of *chessed* that we are familiar with and in relation to Hashem; it is shown by our wanting to give birth to our goodness in any way. It is our desire to go beyond the normal limits in order to bring about more goodness.

---

5 Rabbi Yesha'ayahu HaLevi Horowitz, 1565–1630, known as the SheLaH Hakadosh, after the acronym of the title of his best known work, *Shnei Luchot HaBrit; Vol. 3, Masechet Rosh Hashanah, Torah Ohr, (3)*; "Tekiah hints at the intrinsic straightness which is within man…"
6 *Zohar II, Ki Tetzei, 114;*

Avraham was the first person to do this. This does not mean that the acts that we are familiar with such as his hospitality or his outreach were ends in themselves. He wanted to give of himself and reach out to Hashem. His kindness was his *avodat Hashem*. He wanted to bring Hashem's goodness into the world. This inner desire is the strongest of all our spiritual desires. What we want most is to give expression to our inherent kindness in order to find an address for our inherent capacity for good. This desire is so powerful that it is symbolically called "the right hand."

Therefore, when the *shofar* is blown, we are acknowledging that there is an aspect of Avraham within ourselves. It is the part that wants to bring forth goodness and to connect to Hashem. He wants this even more than we do. He wants to receive us even when we have created obstacles and imperfections.

b) *Shevarim*:

This is a voice that is broken three times. It is the voice of *din* (severity). It is our declaration that we want to break down the barriers that keep us from Hashem. Our will to break down barriers is the voice of Yitzchak. The only meaningful reason to want to break a barrier is that you feel that it is possible and that you truly want to.

As you know the source of all sins is primarily *ga'avah* and *ta'avah*. These traits then give birth to many more subcategories of sins. After doing your *cheshbon nefesh*, you will know what your primary obstacles are. You will then have to be thinking positively, along the lines of "I'm going to get past it"; "I want to move on"; "I want to break down the barriers."

Yitzchak's success in this is almost beyond comprehension. The main barrier is *ga'avah*. Even *ta'avah* (desire or lust) stems from this feeling of Self in its most arrogant and limiting sense, like when you feel that "I deserve this pleasure and should therefore have it, no matter what the price is." Yitzchak's success in breaking through *gaavah* in order to serve only Hashem and not to serve himself was so great that the *Akeidah* was not called his *nisayon*. It was called Avraham's *nisayon* because to

Yitzchak, the battle against ego had long been won. He only wanted to do the Will of Hashem. He never doubted that he could not be killed since the Jewish people were meant to come through him.

c) *Teruah*:

Teruah has elements of both the long voice and the broken voice, in that it is the voice that has to be broken at least nine times. Not only does it have to be of longer duration than the *shevarim* blast, but it has to be even more broken than *shevarim*. This bonding is called *tiferet*. Therefore, there are aspects of both *chessed* and *Gevurah* in the *Teruah* blasts.

There are two *pesukim* that use the word *Teruah* and yet seem to be going in different directions. One is a phrase that comes from the blessings that Bil'am unwittingly gave us when talking about the uniqueness of *Am Yisrael*. He said, "Hashem their G-d is with them, and the *Teruah* (friendship) of their G-d is with them."[7] It is through the actual sound of *Teruah* that Hashem comes toward us. However, there is also a side of *din* in *Teruah*, as it says in *Tehillim*: "to shatter them (using the same root as the word *Teruah*) with the rod of iron." [8]

The ability to unify *chessed* and *gevurah* is called *tiferet* (harmonizing), but is also called "*emet*" and "*rachamim*." The final step of a process always epitomizes the goal of the process. *Tiferet* is the ultimate goal of the other two steps. When you look at a completed building you should be able to understand the intent of the architect when he first drew up the blueprints.

Emet is the whole picture, a picture colored in two shades, one shade being white. There is an enormous light in every person, to the extent that there are times when we feel dazzled by the deeds that these people do. This is because there is so much beauty in their acts.

> I once saw the clip of a boy, Yechiel Davidovich, who was *niftar* a little while ago. Apparently, his parents knew that the one thing that he really wanted was to meet Rav Yitzchak David Grossman. They told

---

7 *Bamidbar* 23:22;
8 *Tehillim* 2:9;

the Rav about the gravity of the child's condition, and the Rav came down from Migdal Ha'emek, which is a very long trip, to see the boy. The clip I saw was of Rabbi Grossman singing to the child. If I personally were to visit an eleven- or twelve-year-old child who was clearly on his deathbed, I wouldn't know what to say. I wouldn't even know what to say to an adult in that condition. The Rav never said a word. He sang. The whole time he sang the Breslever song, "*Abba Chazkeini Techazek et Haneshamah.*" (Father, strengthen me, strengthen my soul). He repeatedly sang the words of *pain, of the struggle*, and you could see it in his eyes. Yet, he was able to bring the child to a place of simchah and love of Hashem. The boy was *niftar* the following day.

In addition to this beautiful dazzling white, the other color that you can see in the world is black. There are things that are horrifying and uninterpretable in the world.

To me, the worst of all of the terrible things I have heard was a story that took place during the war. A woman arrived at a concentration camp with her two children and was told by a Nazi officer that one of her children would be sent to his death. He asked her which one she wanted to save. She realized that if she didn't choose one, the Nazi would immediately shoot both of them in front of her. She therefore chose one...and he killed the other one. That child lived on, knowing that his own mother had chosen him to be the one marked for death. Nothing can describe this in words. The color black says it all.

If *Chessed* Is White and *Gevurah* Is Black, What Are You?

People usually choose to focus on only one color. There are innumerable hues. Most people are predisposed to either always seeing the good, or the bad. *Tiferet* means tapping into the *emet* that the world is comprised of both components and knowing that they are both taking us to the same place. One takes us to *k'vod Shamayim* through meeting the *nisyonot* head-on and having *bitachon* in the face of horror. The other takes us to being inspired by good. This contrast, between the expansiveness of Hashem's *chessed* and the severity of His *din*, are parallel realities that we have to be aware of.

Another word for *tiferet* is *rachamim*. When we see terrible things, they are meant to awaken within us a desire to change them and to do whatever we can, even if all we can do is to cry out to Hashem, "No, Abba, no." That will to change bad things is called *rachamim*, and when *chessed* is added to it, the *tiferet* becomes complete. The natural order, therefore, should be for us to exclaim, "Oh, no," followed by an action to change it. These are the components of both black and white.

Returning to the *Teruah*, this sound is therefore saying to Hashem, "I am broken in many places, but I want more. I want better, I want You." At this point we are seeing both at the same moment, in the same way that a person would see a picture forming through the merger of black and white. This *Teruah* is the middah of Yaakov.

Is Black and White Always Black and White? Can They Be Corrupted?

Avraham gave birth to a Yishmael and Yitzchak gave birth to an Esav. Yishmael was the long voice that wasn't able to find the right direction. He looked around without boundaries, discipline or focus. This is why Yishmael is called *pere adam*, "wild thing that was human."[9] His wildness removed his humanity. Esav, on the other hand, was *Gevurah* gone wild. He wanted to do battle with everything that stood in his way. He was all ego. This is the blood-shedding nature of the Wild West, whose art and literature is saturated with this theme. If you were to remove these elements from their cultural imagery, there would hardly be anything left.

Yaakov Saw Both Black and White. (Overcome What Is Broken, and Elevate What Is Inspired)

Yaakov didn't fail his destiny. His descendants were all perfected. His willingness to see evil and give his children the tools to fight it was what made it possible for him to achieve this. He did it on an individual basis, because every individual has his own inner struggles to contend with. He also allowed them to see the individual forces of good within each

---

9 *Bereishit 16:11–12*

other, as no two forces of good are the same. His ability to see both the good and bad in everything is why he was able to defeat the angel of Esav.

He did this also when he returned to get his small jars, which he felt were important enough for him to recover because they had been given to him to use by Hashem. He recognized that they were meant to be used for *Kedushah* in the same way that everything is meant to be used for good.

Therefore, when we are listening to the *Teruah*, we need to bear in mind that we must deal with and overcome the brokenness within us, and rediscover and elevate the latent goodness that we all possess. This is the voice of Yaakov, which is why we call ourselves "Bnei Yisrael," Yaakov's other name.

What to Concentrate on When You Hear the *Shofar* Blast

Each voice of the *shofar* is meant to evoke a different *kavanah*, which can be substantiated by your own life experience and *cheshbon hanefesh*.

After the brachot are said, the *ba'al korei* will call out the names of each voice that you are hearing. He will call out "Tekiah!" before the *Tekiah* is blown, and "Teruah!" before the *Teruah* is blown. As you hear each voice announced, you need to put yourself in the mindsets you just read about. This has nothing to do with *gashmiut*. Hashem, on His side, will give you the *gashmiut* you need to be a *kli* (vessel) for His *ruchniut*. This is what Yom Din is all about.

Review Before You Go to Shul

The Tekiah mindset. So, when you hear *Tekiah!* announced and are listening to the sound, you will need to be thinking: "I want to express my goodness. I want to see Hashem's goodness," and have in mind to want to see both your goodness and Hashem's goodness.

The Shevarim mindset. When you hear the *Shevarim!* announced, you should envision your will to overcome all the obstacles and to ensure that you know what they are.

The *Teruah mindset.* Then, when you hear *Teruah!* announced, you should think of all of the things you want to do in order to see Hashem's goodness and *kavod.* You should also think that you do not want to see any more terrible things in the world, and can even have in mind some actual events that you know have occurred in recent times. You should focus on how you want to see goodness and Mashiach.

Rosh Hashanah is the Yom Hadin specifically for *gashmiut,* but the *gashmiut* is sent down to fit the *ruchniut.* The *shofar* sound is meant to bring you to a place where your *ruchniut* is ready to receive the *gashmiut* that Hashem will send you.

The Core of the Longest Service of the Year

The most important tefillah in terms of capturing the essence of Rosh Hashanah is Mussaf. Mussaf has four sections: The *Korban*[10], *Malchuyot, Zichronot* and *Shofarot.*

1) *Malchuyot*

The purpose of *Malchuyot* is to bring *k'vod Hashem* into the world. Therefore in the tefillot, we precede *Malchuyot* with statements in the machzor about how much we desire to see Hashem's *malchut* in the world. The pesukim are from the Torah, *Nevi'im,* and *Ketuvim.* They are used to teach us where this *tefillah* is meant to direct us, and are concepts that we would never figure out on our own.

Some of the pesukim and their central ideas:

Hashem yimloch l'olam va'ed[11] – When you are saying this, you are saying that all time was created with purpose. This purpose is *k'vod Shamayim,* and *time* refers to all the events of the past and of the future. *Malchuyot* means taking events as they unfold and dedicating them to Hashem.

Hashem malach gei'ut lavesh (finding Hashem in Nature[12]) – The passuk tells us that Hashem rules, and His garment is *gaavah.* The splendor of nature, along with its beauty and intricacy, has profound hidden power.

---

10 *see page 74 for an in-depth explanation of the korban;*
11 *Shemot 15:8;*
12 *Tehillim 93:1;*

Rambam tells us that according to Halachah, "a person is obligated to meditate a moment before he davens the Shemoneh Esrei." The idea of being *mitbonen* is tied to what tefillah should arouse within you, namely, the awareness of the intricacy and beauty of everything you see around you.

An illustration of how the impact that this should have within you internally is evident from an experience that one of my students went through. She finished Neve and got a real-world job in Manhattan. She was a very low-level cog in a huge corporate machine.

She found herself in this gigantic room where many other people were working in cubicles that were separated by tiny partitions. One day she was working and received a memo that she needed to go up to the Big Boss. She certainly wasn't expecting this, so she thought that it was a mistake and went to tell her supervisor about it. The supervisor told her that it was not a mistake, as it had the company seal on it. Therefore, he told her that she had to go.

She knew how small her position was, so she felt that if this wasn't a mistake, then she must have done something really, dreadfully wrong. She even considered just going home and letting go of the job. But she didn't and instead went to the information officer who guided her to the special elevator that was used only to take people to the offices of the most senior members of the company. She went into the elevator assuming that when the doors opened, she would find herself in a long corridor that would lead her to an office. However, the elevator opened into a huge room with a beautiful carpet and a mahogany desk where her highness, the receptionist was seated.

The receptionist then asked, "How may I help you?" in a condescending tone, as she obviously believed that the girl had arrived there by accident. The girl showed her the memo and was ushered immediately into the inner chamber. The office was huge, with good art and a wall that was all window with an exquisite view. The boss then asked her to sit down and said, "I asked my secretary to speak to someone in Human Resources to find me a practicing Orthodox Jew. I want to ask you a question, because I want to know what an average Orthodox Jew thinks. Would you mind answering the question for me?"

She obviously responded "No," and he asked her, "I can see from my office into the synagogue, and I can see that the men are on the ground floor and the women are on the balcony above. I was just wondering what that is about? Why are the women higher than the men?" She answered whatever she answered, but the important factor here is what she was feeling at that moment. She was scared. This executive wasn't even worthy of standing in the presence of her Rabbi. He was nothing, no one in the eternal scheme of things. But still, his outward grandeur and the way in which people regarded him brought about a certain awe.

A way in which this kind of awe is expressed is when you bow during Shemoneh Esrei. The Ariza"l[13] says (and this view is presented in Mishneh Brurah as the halachah) that the bowing should be quick, because if you really let yourself think about in Whose presence you are standing, you wouldn't be able to stand erect at the end of it – the bowing would be instinctive, immediate. You should perceive Hashem's greatness and use it to inform you of your smallness.

2) *Zichronot* (Remembrance)

Hashem remembers every thought, deed and word that we uttered over the course of the entire year. Nothing has been forgotten. This is a terrifying thought, and yet the theme in *Zichronot* does not stress this point. Instead, we talk about all the positive events that Hashem remembers, beginning with Noah and Hashem's covenant with him. Toward the end there is a passuk that states that "Hashem remembers Ephraim."[14] Ephraim was one of the first tribes to be forced out of Eretz Yisrael because of the incessant idol worship that the ten tribes had turned into a lifestyle. Yet when we recite what Hashem remembers, Hashem says of this tribe "I remember that you are my precious child, the child whom I played with. I remember my love for you. When I talk about you, I yearn for you."

---

13 *Sha'ar HaKavanot of Rav Chaim Vital in the name of the Ariza"l;*
14 *Yirmiyahu 31:19; 'Is Ephraim My most precious son…whenever I speak of him I remember him more and more. Therefore My inner self yearns for him, I will surely have compassion for him…"*

It is very important for us to remember that this is the nature of Hashem's *zikaron*. Rav Moshe Cordovero (the RaMaK) in *Tomer Devorah* discusses how Hashem relates to our sins. Words that usually come to our mind in this regard are generally those that convey rage, and indeed these are words of Torah. That is how Hashem acts toward us, but we need to be aware of where He is coming to us, from the inside.

Hashem is with you – you never suffer alone. There is a passuk in *Yesha'yahu* that contains the phrase: "in all of their suffering."[15] The word used there is *lo tzar*. The meaning of *lo* varies depending on its spelling, and could mean either "no" or "to Him." Here it is written one way, but is meant to be read another. This is a technique known as *kri uch'tiv* and is found all over *Tanach*. The way it's written here is with an aleph (meaning no), but is read with a vav (meaning to Him). This means that the passuk is written to be understood as "in all of our suffering, it doesn't hurt Him." We caused this suffering to fall upon ourselves through our own efforts. We make our own choices. But when the passuk is read aloud it is as if saying, "in all of our suffering, He suffers."

The way you read a word (if it is different from the way it's spelled) has to do with what is not observable, and *ktiv* (spelling) is connected to reality as we see it.

It is often observable in the world that we sometimes make terrible mistakes and then have to live with the consequences, whether they are in relation to the way we affected other people or in relation to our own lives. This is a responsibility that we hold both as a people and as individuals. This is evident from the *Divrei Habrit*[16], which delineate all the actions that will generate specific consequences, sometimes with terrible, horrific results. We have seen this in our history. It is all true. When our mind's eye is focused there, we don't see Hashem's love for us.

However, if we look beneath the surface in order to discover the motivation for His judgments, we will see that the purpose is *tikkun*.

---

15 *Yesha'yahu 63:9;*
16 *Devarim 28:69, referring to chapters 27–30;*

This idea can be understood through the following slightly altered story. I was once in an exercise class where the participants were either women over fifty or young girls. The class sort of self-divided toward the end, with the young girls all on the floor following the instructions of the instructor who was saying things like, "OK, girls, now wind your ankle around your neck and sit up." At this point, two other women and I were sitting on a bench, waiting for the hour to pass. One of the women started saying, "You know, soon we're having a simchah in our family. There is going to be a *pidyon haben*. It's been over half a century since there was a *pidyon haben* in my husband's family." The other woman began to cry.

I had about a split-second to decide whether I should notice or not notice this. I wasn't sure how to best respond. I could have kept silent, assuming that whatever this evoked was private, or I could have asked what happened and given her the opportunity to say something. Even now I am still not sure whether I did the right thing. I decided to ask her what happened, thinking that if she didn't feel like speaking, she would just say "Nothing, nothing," and I would act like it was a normal thing. She answered that when she heard the words *firstborn child*, she remembered what was happening with her own firstborn son. Her son, within a few short weeks, due to a number of misunderstandings, had moved from being an excellent student in a much respected yeshiva to being a waiter in Tel Aviv. Her feelings here were those of grief.

This would be a good way of describing Hashem's feelings, so to speak. He does what He has to do. He sees how we self-destruct and how deeply we dig our holes. He then throws a rope down to us, and this rope is called *tikkun*. He will do for and to us whatever is needed in order for *tikkun* to take place. But He is with us. This is what we need to remember and hold on to on Rosh Hashanah. We need to remember that "You remember all the deeds, even in the midst of that evil You made the world survive."[17] The world continued after the flood although it functioned on a different level.

---

17 The Complete Artscroll Machzor – Rosh Hashanah, pg. 461; '…the remembrance of all deeds comes before You…remembering Noah with love…[even] as You brought the waters of the Flood to destroy all…because of the evil of their deeds."

Zichronot is supposed to then lead us to tell Hashem that He remembers our yearning for Him, as well as all of the mistakes that we have made. We are asking Him to remember that underneath it all, He knows who we are and what we want. This evokes great mercy.

3) *Shofarot*

The main topic in *Shofarot* is *Matan Torah*.[18] This takes us back to the main *kavanah* for all of *shofar* blowing that we hear. Namely, that when the Torah was given, we were completely "there." We had the desire for good, the willingness to accept what is difficult in order to overcome obstacles, and we were willing to see the *emet*. We therefore need to accept and acknowledge that we will do what Hashem wants of us.

This is the physical expression of our acceptance of Hashem's *Malchuyot*.

---

18 *Shemot, 19:16 – 19; ibid. 20·15;*

SHIUR 5

How to Emerge from Yom Kippur Cleansed and Changed by the Tefillot

The days between Rosh Hashanah, and Yom Kippur are the Aseret Yemei Teshuvah, which in some ways are the most significant days of the entire year. At this time, we are told to "seek Hashem from where He can be found."[1] Hashem of course can be found anywhere. The question therefore is, how should we go about making the Ten Days of Repentance different from any other time?

The answer is that the Aseret Yemei Teshuvah are a time when all of the work that we have been discussing until this point needs to be actualized. There are four ways in which this occurs. The most central is saying *Viduy* when we admit to Hashem that we have sinned. *Viduy* is the culmination of all of the other forms of Teshuvah, as it is the only part of Teshuvah that is *mi-d'Oraisa* (Torah derived).

Now is the time that you will complete the process of teshuvah that you began. The days between Rosh Hashanah and Yom Kippur are days when you can practice being the person that you want to be for the rest of your life. You can't become a finished product, but you can begin walking up the ladder. You have to start - otherwise you end up with your feet stuck on the ground. The starting steps have to be real, defined, and small enough to be practical.

Rabbeinu Yonah[2] explains to us that there are four steps required for Teshuvah to occur. Two of them are related to the past, and the other two are focused on the present and future.

---

1 *Yesha'yahu*, 55:6;
2 "The Gates of Repentance" (*Sha'arei Teshuva*)

Articulation of the *Viduy*

There are two big misconceptions that might arise when a person is saying *Viduy*. One is to transform it into an intellectual exercise. Sometimes, you can use a book on teshuvah to compile a list of all of the deeds that you did wrong, but somehow it remains academic. If you want any enduring and real change to take place, you have to bring your feelings back into the picture. The ability to make it enter your heart is the *ikkar*.

The other mistake is that when you open your heart to what you are reading/saying, you can find it so painful and embarrassing that you decide to take a break because it is too overwhelming. You end up distracting yourself with anything that gives you the option of not thinking (this includes holiday shopping, exploring meal options, reading moving and touching stories about other people's teshuvah, etc.) All of this is good. The problem arises only when you are so absorbed with the externals of the holiday that you let it replace the inner side. This is a normal feeling, but it is not constructive.

The solution is to make Hashem your trusted mentor.

> There is a good approach outlined in Machshavah by Rabbi Yaakov Ades, wherein he explains it in terms of going to a therapist. The first step is to call the therapist and make an appointment, realizing that it will cost you serious money. When you have entered her room, at that point all you are going to do is tell her your problem. If you find yourself focusing on how long it took to get to her office, how much the cab cost, or how much you like her waiting room décor, you are wasting your money. You are clearly not ready for therapy.

Similarly, when you are saying *Viduy*, you need to picture Hashem before you and He is saying, "What brings you here today?" Your answer, then, is "*Ashamnu*, I did this and this and this, and I am not sure that I am out of it or how to get out of it, and this is where I am." This is what *Viduy* is about; identifying your problems and taking them to Hashem. Take them to Hashem and tell Him that you need His intervention. The fact that you have done the sin, and that you keep returning to it, tells you that you absolutely must go for help, and this help needs to come from Above.

Rabbi Yaakov then tells us that when we are asking Hashem for help in this way, the next step is to realize that if you take the conventional steps of Teshuvah and open yourself to some degree to asking for help, then you are basically there.

In shul, when you are saying one of the five *Viduys* recited on Yom Kippur, ideally you will be focusing on this idea of appealing to your Therapist for help in all of these areas. However, all of the inner work regarding why you are doing these actions and how you could possibly combat them, should have been done prior to this. Elul is the time for doing the best you can to be really ready for these big moments of authentic intimacy with Hashem.

You wonder why the same words are repeated so many times. Basically, each time you say *Viduy* you are asking for the same things, but at each of these points, *Viduy* is accompanied by different tefillot, which are meant to reframe the way you look at the world, at yourself and your deeds.

Erev Yom Kippur. The custom is to say *Viduy* before you eat, in case you should choke while you are eating (*chas v'shalom*). This may seem a bit strange, as most people do not choke while they are eating. The real point of this action is to help us gain awareness of human mortality and also attach the *Viduy* to real life, because you are about to sit down to eat a meal. Even though this is a normal act, you really don't know what will happen in the next moment, and you don't want to die with these things on your heart.

Maariv (Aravit). In Maariv you would be feeling the darkness and groping in it, whereas in Shacharit, it is the exact opposite. Being able to say *Viduy* when you don't as yet see the light breaking and turning night into day, is a profound statement of faith in Hashem's presence and His love for us.[3]

---

3 See *Tehillim*, 92:3 "*It is good to thank HaShem…to speak of Your kindnesses at dawn and Your faithfulness in the nights.*"

I was once in Prague for several days. I went on a guided trip to There-sienstadt. It had been a sort of static horror house in which Jews were "stored" until they could be sent east to their destruction. The hellish conditions led to many fatalities. There was a crematorium to take "care" of the extra corpses before they could accumulate. There was also a hidden basement that the inmates turned into a tiny sacred space in which they could pray. One of them wrote on the wall a famous line from the Tachanun prayers that are recited Mondays and Thursdays: "In spite of it all, we have not forgotten Your Name."[4] The man who wrote this had faith in the darkest of all places. He, no doubt, was imperfect, just like the rest of us, but that didn't take him to despair (but instead, might have played out by his saying, "G-d is concealed, but I am here. I will seek Him and not let my past mistakes lead me to despair.")

Shacharit. At Shacharit you are most cognizant of Hashem's dominion and the intricacy of His creation. The intent here should be that you are asking Hashem to pull you out of your present reality. You ask Him to recall the deeds and traits of the partriarchs, your genetic spiritual ancestors, and implore Him to look at you and see that part of them that is still alive deep within you. You want to tap into their spiritual brilliance and dazzling compassion.

Mussaf is always about the *korban* of the day, although we will not be exploring this in depth here. The nature of a *korban* is to find the part of your animal soul that responds to the *korban*, for instance, by identifying with the sheep or ram in you, and so on. You then need to take this awareness and consecrate it to the service of Hashem. Your *Viduy* in Mussaf confronts you with where your animal self has led you. It simultaneously tells you, "Now you can turn it around," and use the very same energy for the good.

Minchah was Yitzchak Avinu's *tikkun*, the idea being that at precisely the time when you are in the middle of your daily activities, you stop what you are doing in order to recognize Hashem in the midst of your busiest moments. These are the times when you may sometimes forget

---

4 The Complete Artscroll Siddur, *Tachanun, pg. 135;*

the bigger picture. When you think back to those moments and say *Viduy*, you have taken a step toward confronting your tendency to be so focused on your need to get things done that you forget why you are here to begin with.

Ne'ilah. Now that you know that the gates are closing, you grasp the last moments of the holiest day of the year to pour your heart out to Hashem, and ask Him to make your Teshuvah stick.

Does this sound like a great deal of focus? It is. This is why you start now, in Elul, rather than leaving it all for the actual day of Yom Kippur.

Asking Hashem for Help in Actualizing Your Teshuvah

This occurs after the *cheshbon hanefesh.* Now you are asking Hashem for help in changing a middah, either by redirecting the middah or by altering the negative energy inherent in the middah. You are therefore going beyond deed into middah.

Another aspect of the past is *charatah* (regret), which has a terrible reputation as it implies a great deal of guilt. True *charatah*, as opposed to random guilt and bad feelings, is when you allow yourself to experience the fact that you have suffered a loss. Sometimes you need to appeal to Hashem for the *siyatta diShmaya* to feel this loss, and conversely, to feel the pleasure of doing what is right, such as by saying a brachah with the correct *kavanah.* If the action is related to something that was done to someone else and there truly is nothing you can do to rectify it, then it's possible that all you can do is appeal to Hashem for the *siyatta diShmaya* to behave differently in the future should a similar incident arise again. You are not asking for a challenge, but for an opportunity.

For instance, imagine that you were downtown and discovered that you were pickpocketed. You find that the money that should have been in your wallet isn't there. The distress you feel will depend on the amount that is missing. A 25-shekel loss is annoying, but it won't eat you up alive. But, if you were planning on buying an expensive item, it is a completely different feeling. Missing $2,000 is very different from missing $5.

Similarly, at this point, you need to ask yourself what you are missing because of the sin. You then need to calculate exactly what is missing. In order to do this, you need to realize what the effect of sin is. Whenever you make a moral choice, no matter how minor it seems to be, it leaves an impression upon you. If you do a good deed, for instance overcoming the temptation to tell a defensive lie, you end up stronger than you were before the temptation raised its ugly head. The impression made by your choosing truth stays with you long after the incident is forgotten.

Let's say that you made a bad choice: you told the lie! It isn't as if you were afraid you would be caught. If you realistically felt that you'd be discovered, no doubt you wouldn't have told the lie to begin with. If everything went as planned, you'd get away with the lie in the short run. Nevertheless, the impression of having "succeeded" leaves its mark. The next time you are tempted to lie, you are more likely to just go for it. When you succeed, you are in danger. The danger is that you will bear the *roshem* (impression) of your success. You know that you can lie and get away with it. All of the "workers" of the yetzer hara operate on an emotional level, not a rational one. Therefore, since the motivation of all sins is based on the assumption that by doing the act, you will derive some form of pleasure from it, you know that if you didn't derive pleasure, you wouldn't do it.

Picture the following scenario: You feel that someone has embarrassed you, perhaps because she gossiped about you and there is enough half-truth in it that it is credible. In such a situation, it is natural to want to defend yourself. You may say, "You know, I've heard that so-and-so is saying this and this, I don't know the story, but that's how she is. She is very defensive because of her own feelings of insecurity." People buy into what you are saying because it is true. When you see on people's faces that they believe you, you feel very good. If it didn't feel very good, you wouldn't have done it.

However, this action has taught you something: that being successfully reactive feels very good. That impression is now implanted. This pleasure isn't self-deceptive but true.

To take this a little bit further, we can see that the above case has its roots in *ga'avah*, as so many do.

Now that you are committed to change, you can focus on the specific roots of your errors in order to avoid dealing with your sins "cosmetically" and making only surface changes.

The three kinds of Sins: cheit, avon, and pesha.

a) *Cheit – A sin done through negligence.* A sin done through negligence isn't what it seems. You transgress because your sense of values isn't that solid.

> Envision a man who boards a flight from New York to Chicago at 12:00 in the afternoon on Friday. The flight should take around three hours, so he plans to arrive there at about 15:00 with Shabbos coming in at 17:00. This should work out, as it only takes around half an hour to reach his destination from the airport. However, those of us who travel know that this isn't likely. You can never count on travel connections going smoothly. There are all sorts of delays that can occur with luggage or departure time or on the highway. With these factors in mind, it's possible that he could only arrive at his destination with 15 seconds to spare, or even 15 minutes after candle lighting. Either way, at this stage he has done a sin *b'shogeg* (accidentally). He wasn't planning on breaking Shabbos, but he put himself in a situation where there was a strong possibility of this occurring. This is a sin that results from negligence rather than intention. The problem here is that on his scales of values, Shabbos wasn't high enough, otherwise he never would have taken that chance.

There are things that you would never take a chance on, like taking medicine for a heart condition. If the doctor tells you to take half a tablet daily, you would never take two tablets because you would have paid careful attention to his words, especially if he expressed how dangerous it was. Therefore, in a situation such as the one above, you need to ask yourself truthfully what was really going on. If you find yourself in such a situation, you need to question why Shabbos wasn't really that important to you.

The loss is there, even if you arrived where you meant to with a minute to spare, so technically, you didn't desecrate Shabbos. The fact is that rather than panicking about how close you came to desecrating Shabbos, you probably feel relieved that everything worked out alright. You have just created a *roshem* that "I can do what I want and it is OK, because it will work out at the very last second." This is not how you would have felt if you had taken four times the medication you should have taken and had not died. You would not have said, "OK, that's good, so now I know that I can take four times the amount of medication." Rather, you would have said to yourself 'Oh my, I could have died!'

STOP READING RIGHT HERE! ASK YOURSELF, "WHAT ARE MY CORE VALUES?" HAVE I REALLY BEEN FAITHFUL TO THEM?"

b) *Avon – the sin of desire.* These are sins that come from a place wherein you derive physical pleasure. They come from the body, meaning that you place your physical needs above your spiritual needs. An illustration of this is where you are shopping and you find an outfit that looks really good on you. It is the right color and cut for you, but you realize that while it covers your knees when standing, it probably doesn't cover your knees when sitting.

> I was actually once in a dress shop in America where the proprietor had a chair in her changing room that invited the customer to sit down in front of the mirror to see how the garment looked when you sit. Now, imagine yourself in this situation where there is a chair and no notice on the wall to provide you with an outside voice. You look in the mirror and you see that it covers your knees when you are standing, but you don't try sitting down. You need to ask yourself honestly what is in it for you when you don't sit down. You can't claim ignorance, because we have all seen how a skirt rides up when a woman sits down in a skirt that is a bit short. But, what is in it for you is that you get to have the dress that you desire.

STOP AGAIN! ASK YOURSELF, "HAVE I MADE HARD CHOICES THIS YEAR? WHAT CAN I DO TO SEE THAT I KEEP ON WINNING WHEN I DO BATTLE WITH MYSELF?"

Here, the *roshem* created is the good feeling you have whenever you put that dress on. After all, there is no bolt of lightning that comes to strike you down when you wear it. Therefore, the *roshem* of *avon* (the impression this sin leaves on you) is the pleasure derived from certain actions and sometimes even the prestige or attention you derive from these behaviours.

c) *Pesha – a sin of rebellion.* This comes about when you feel that your ego is diminished in some way, either by another person or even by Hashem. This could be through someone doing or saying something that embarrasses you or makes you feel bad about yourself. This is therefore a reaction to strengthen your sense of self-preservation.

I once read a horrific article in a religious women's magazine about the artificial expectations of what parenting should be. These include expectations that parents have to provide children with unconditional love and support and that they should speak only kindly and nicely to them in spite of the fact that the children aren't perfect. This creates expectations that cannot be fulfilled and leads to a great deal of anger against parents.

In this article, the following situation was presented:

A young daughter got married, moved to live near her mother and came to visit her parents frequently for meals. The mother expects her to pitch in a little bit, but doesn't say so explicitly out of fear of losing her child's affection. One day the mother has to leave the house, and when she returns, she finds her five-year-old writhing on the floor in pain. The adult daughter is in the living room reading a book, ignoring the child. The mother then scoops up the child and tries to comfort him, but when she sees that this isn't working, she takes him to the emergency room and discovers that he needs an emergency appendectomy.

The daughter's husband called up later and shouted at the mother for being angry with the daughter and scolding her. The resolution in the article was that the mother should try to appease the daughter and son-in-law!

Why was the son-in-law angry? His guilt made him feel small. He needed to blame someone for what happened. This always happens when a person feels small and helpless. If you have "tapes" of relieving your anger by blaming someone, by lying, or any other means of assuaging guilt, like the son-in-law in the story, you are much more likely to use the same tool again.

From this perspective, the impression that the sin leaves on your subconscious can be more destructive than the deed itself. There are all sorts of impressions that leave their mark on a person. Each of them has a defined beginning.

The impressions left and already written in your subconscious diary:

a) physical pleasures;

b) feelings of self-significance;

c) knowledge that you got away with murder (okay, maybe not murder, but lots of other things that you know very well are wrong);

The assumptions you make about life are sometimes false. How do you erase the messages you have been busy engraving on your subconscious? The only thing that can counteract the years and years of misinterpretation of reality, is the closeness to Hashem that you get when you do Teshuvah.

STOP ONE FINAL TIME. ASK YOURSELF ABOUT HOW YOU RESPONDED TO FEELING SMALL OR GUILTY THIS PAST YEAR. WERE YOU DEFENSIVE? TO WHOM DO YOU FEEL THAT YOU NEED TO DEFEND YOURSELF? WHY? HOW CAN YOU CHANGE THINGS THIS COMING YEAR?

A Serious Desire for a Different Behavior

This is the step that involves the present, as it requires you to change the deed and to do the inner work.

What if you don't want to want? If you do not seriously want to change your behavior, this indicates a lack of awareness of the great distance this behavior is taking you from your relationship with Hashem. In the

end, a distance from Hashem means that there is also a distance from your higher self and from your desire to achieve these heights.

If you are not at the point of wanting to change these behaviors, you lack the motivation to change. Therefore, the first step is to get to the point where you sincerely want something different.

As we mentioned earlier, wanting to change requires having a plan. Vague ideas of wanting to be different are not a plan. This again brings us back to the process that we discussed earlier in connection with making your *cheshbon hanefesh* where you get to the middah and find a way to redirect it. This plan needs to work from the inside out, because once you change the middah, the deed will change.

According to *Chazal*, there are times when we have to change from the outside in, but there are not always clear ways in which to do this. You would need this method sometimes because every time you perform the deed, you are strengthening the *roshem*. This is especially true in *avonot* from which you get considerable pleasure. So, in the case of a person who wears immodest clothing or eats dubious *hechsherim*, the *roshem* of the physical pleasure is strengthened. As a result of this, you absolutely need to start from the outside in or else you will fail at every attempt to change the middah from the inside. Instead, the problem will just increase. Be willing to work on the problem from the outside-in, at least as a first step.

It is possible, depending on your personality, that you will also need to apply this method to sins related to the other areas as well.

The basic equation is that the more addictive the sin is, the more likely you need to begin completely from the outside in order not to create a situation where real change is impossible.

Part of the plan, as outlined by Rav Yaakov Ades, is to question not only what is going on inside you when you do the wrong thing, but to assess where you are and what is going on outside of you at the time. He says that there are actual places that lead a person in the wrong direction.

A simplistic example of this is going to a reunion. You know yourself well enough to be aware that you have big issues with lashon hara and that going to a reunion would not be a good idea, because it is not a place where people wouldn't speak about others. Therefore, it might be better to either not go or to only remain for a short time. It may also be a good idea to just hang out with the *tzaddeikes* of the class.

There are places that inherently produce temptations and you cannot maintain that you have an honest desire to change if you are sabotaging yourself. With that in mind, then, you need to assess what the place is and what the deeds are. For most people, there needs to be some level of *shiluv*, or "joining together two things that are separate." Here the *shiluv* is the merging of the deed and the inner work. However, there are no formulas and there can't be formulas. This is because every person is different, and every person's life circumstances are different.

Guarding Against Lost Opportunities in the Future

This step is based on the future, which is of course built on the past and the present.

Once I heard a story which made a deep impression on me: I have a house guest who comes to visit me once a year. In deference to what she wanted we went to daven at a Sephardic shul in Har Nof, even though I would not generally do so on Shabbos because of the differences in *nusach*. However, this worked out very well for me, because I always go to speak at Neve Yerushalayim on Shabbos Teshuvah, which always bothers me as I don't really want to listen to myself speak on this day. I would prefer to hear somebody express an idea that I do not already know.

As it worked out, Rav Ovadya's son Rav David Yosef decided to speak in the morning. In his drashah, he asked a question regarding the *gemara*[5] that tells us that when Moshe was in heaven receiving the Torah from Hashem, Hashem showed him that in the future, there would be someone who would be able to explain all of the *kitrei otiot*, the lines (crowns) protruding from the letters. Moshe then asks Hashem who this would be, and Hashem says, "Rabbi Akiva," and then shows him a scene of Rabbi Akiva teaching his students. Moshe is amazed because he

---

5 *Talmud Bavli, Menachot 29b;*

sees that Rabbi Akiva knows things that Moshe does not know. Moshe is then consoled when a student asks Rabbi Akiva a question, and Rabbi Akiva responds that he does not know. The student says, "We do it even though we don't know why?" to which Rabbi Akiva responds, "This is what I received from Moshe Rabbeinu from Har Sinai."

However, Moshe was left with a question. He saw who this man was, but then asked what his reward would be in this world, because the reward in this world is never the final reward and punishment, it is simply the means of going further. Hashem then showed him that after Rabbi Akiva's horrific death, his flesh was sold to the Romans in the public market. Moshe then said 'This is Torah, and this is its reward?" Hashem responded, "Be silent because this is what I have decided."

This is obviously a very painful and puzzling story. Rabbi David Yosef explained that in order to understand this story, we must first refer to an earlier *gemara* that tells us about Hillel.[6]

The *gemara* says that Hillel obligates the poor, because when a person appears before Hashem and tells Him that the reason that he did not behave as properly as he might have was because of his poverty, which subtracted a great deal of his time from Torah study, Hashem will show him Hillel. Hillel was incredibly poor and one day did not have enough money to gain entry to the *beit medrash,* so he climbed onto the roof to listen at the sky light, and nearly froze to death.

It is possible for a poor person to look at this story of Hillel and say that this does not obligate him at all, because all he has in common with Hillel is his poverty, not his intellectual gifts or spiritual sensitivity. After all, Hillel lived a hundred years before the destruction of the Temple. The people he saw every day and the people that the poor person sees every day are completely different. Hillel was the *Rebbe* of Rabbi Yochanan ben Zakkai. How could there be any comparison? Therefore, the only basis for this comparison is that Hillel actualized his potential in spite of his poverty, and this poor person could also emerge from his poverty as his maximized self, not as a person who is defined by his limitations.

---

6 *Talmud Bavli, Yoma 35b;*

Let us take this back to another period in Rabbi Akiva's life, when he was a student of Rabbi Eliezer Hagadol, whose quality of retaining his learning is compared to "a sealed cistern that doesn't lose a drop"[7]. When Rabbi Eliezer didn't accept the decisions of Rabban Gamliel, he was put into *cheirem* (excommunicated) in order to preserve the unity of Klal Yisrael. He spent many years in *cheirem*, during which time he didn't leave his home, which must be excruciatingly painful for one who wants to teach. After Rabban Gamliel's death, when it was clear that Rabbi Eliezer's life was coming to an end, the sages of the time went to visit him, which was permitted as it was not done in the face of Rabban Gamliel's authority. They wished to perform the ceremony to nullify the *cheirem* in order that they could speak with him. When they arrived, he asked them why they had come. They said, "In order to learn from you." He said, "You are coming [only] now?" to which they answered, "Yes." He then cursed them and wished upon them that they all die difficult deaths. Rabbi Akiva, who was his student, asked him, "Even me?" – and he said, "You shall have the worst."[8]

This is a very difficult story. He responded in this way because it was possible for them to have annulled the *cheirem* earlier, and the *cheirem* had prevented them from learning and integrating what they could have learned from him. This missed opportunity to grow caused a deep lack of development. In the case of Rabbi Akiva, when he met his very painful death, he told his students, "This is what I always wanted, to be able to serve Hashem with all of my soul."[9] This means that his death was what was missing in him. Whatever spiritual lack he had within him was atoned for through the trials of his physical death.

7 *Pirkei Avot, 2:9*
8 *Talmud Bavli, Berachot 19a; Shabbat 130b; Bava Metzia 59b*
9 *Talmud Bavli, Berachot 61b;*

This story comes to teach us that when we are planning for the future, we should have in mind not to allow any opportunity for growth to slip by. Hashem is invested in all of us and wants us to be maximized.

We also need to be aware that our Teshuvah can't erase a *roshem*. The erasure of a *roshem* stems from the *siyatta diShmaya* that our Teshuvah brings down. Teshuvah brings down the *siyatta diShmaya* that brings us closer to Hashem. Therefore, the main focus of Yom Kippur is to bring down the *siyatta diShmaya* that we will need to effect real change. On your own, you don't have the capacity to effect change, but only to want it. This feeling should then produce simchah in your heart as Yom Kippur is meant to be a very happy day.

This is comparable to a person who is very ill and is experiencing an excessive amount of suffering, and so goes to see a doctor. The doctor gives him some medication to take, and the pain disappears. In the case of a diabetic whose sugar balance is completely off and gets found wandering the streets and behaving and he is then taken to a hospital where he is given something to drink and immediately reverts back to himself; this is teshuvah.

The Maharal tells us that Teshuvah is a miraculous cure that fixes you.[10] In order to maximize the potential for rectification, one therefore needs to do one's best to stay focused on one's davening and the purpose of the day.

---

10 Netivot HaTeshuvah, chapter 3;

Yom Kippur – A Unique Opportunity

We also need to keep our eyes open for the opportunities that Hashem presents us with to fix these areas that we are appealing to Him for on Yom Kippur. Therefore, if we are asking Him to help us become a *ba'al chessed*, we need to work at paying attention to and fulfilling any *chessed* opportunities that present themselves.

Rambam quotes Rabbi Yishmael in Hilchot Teshuvah. Rabbi Yishmael tells us that Yom Kippur has a completely different level of *Kedushah* from the rest of the year. He tells us that when we sinned intentionally, even if we did Teshuvah during the year, the only way that we can atone fully is through the cleansing purity of the *siyatta diShmaya* that is only available on Yom Kippur.[11] Yom Kippur is unique and unlike any other day of the year.

Shanah Tovah!
May it be a good and blessed Year for all of Klal Yisrael
and may we merit to see Mashiach speedily and in our days.
Amen.

---

11 *Avot D'Rabi Natan 29; regarding what Rabbi Yishmael used to teach with regard to the four categories of atonement;*

APPENDIX

Description of the Thirteen Attributes of Mercy

The following explanation of the *middos harachamim* is taken from the classic Sefer, *Tomer Devorah* by Harav Moshe Cordevero.

Because we are created in G-d's image, we have to learn the traits that make us more similar to our Creator. This similarity is not meant to be vague or "spiritual" (in the ungrounded sense of the word). *Kedushah* is meant to be real, concrete, and definable. The prophets didn't add any new mitzvot to the Torah. Their role was to take the concepts of the Torah and "color" them human.

Micha[1] says: "Who is a force like You, Who carries sins of desire, and passes over sins of rebellion to the remainder of His inheritance? He does not hold on to His anger forever, because His desire is kindness. He shall return and have compassion upon us, conquer our sins, and toss all our sins into the depths of the sea. You shall give truth to Yaakov, kindness to Avraham as You promised to our Fathers in the earliest times." These sentences articulate the thirteen attributes of Hashem's mercy.

Who is a force like You … Hashem is strong enough to be a King who can "afford" to allow Himself to suffer insult; He is not vulnerable. Because of this, He sustains even those who sin, even as they sin. This is meant to give us a goal in our own lives; this goal is being willing to bear with people, and strong enough not to need to "defend ourselves" constantly.

Who bears sins … Hashem is willing to take on Himself the responsibility to "deal" with situations that we create. He saves us from the logical outcomes of our sins. He is waiting either for Teshuvah to take place, or for the sinner's suffering to open his eyes and cause him to change, or for him to receive his atonement in Gehennom. This trait is meant to inspire us to let things proceed as Hashem wishes.

---

1 7:18–20

He passes over intended sins...Hashem directly involves Himself in our process of Teshuvah and deals with us directly. This should make us feel ashamed of our sins, knowing that Hashem Himself is fully aware of our need to be cleansed.

To the remnant of His inheritance...Hashem sees us as an extension of Himself; in the same way we should be able to be broad enough to feel responsible for every other Jew as though he is a blood relative.[2]

He does not hold on to His anger forever...Hashem does not have an "all-or-nothing" relationship to us. Even when we sin, He maintains His relationship with us. That fact notwithstanding, the relationship is not reciprocal. Humans have to learn to write their own script and not just respond to other people's faults and failings by "answering" with their own defensiveness. This is relevant especially when we are right!

Because He loves kindness...Hashem loves doing *chessed* for us and waits for us to do *chessed* with each other, which will open the door to receive *chessed* from Him. Therefore, look for opportunities to help others even if they are not perfect. Love them and be kind to them for who they are.

He returns and has compassion...Unlike a human who gets tired of giving (the 'Why don't you just buy yourself your own stepladder?' syndrome), Hashem enjoys giving. This is especially true when someone tries to do Teshuvah repeatedly. At some point the person will be ashamed to keep on saying, "I'm sorry." Hashem's greatest gift is forgiveness, and He truly takes pleasure in giving. Similarly, humans should at least stop enjoying opportunities for "teaching someone a lesson" by taking revenge.

He conquers our sins...Even when a person commits a terrible sin, one that no human could forgive under any circumstances, Hashem will not let the sin block out whatever good that person has done. He will reward the good and not let the sin erase it. You may have good reason

---

2 *quoted in the name of the REM"A, Rav Menachem Azariah de Fano, 16th century Italian posek and kabbalist; disciple of Rabbi Cordevero.*

to despise someone, but if he has done you a favor, that still must be recalled and repaid.

He throws their sins into the depths of the sea...Because of Hashem's love for us, when we need to be confronted with who we are in contrast to who we should be, He often sends us enemies to bring us back to knowing who we are and who we want to be. These enemies, such as Pharaoh, are punished because of their choice-making process, even though the results were ultimately for our benefit. He does not, however, use a Jew as his "stick" to punish. Therefore if you see a Jewish person suffering because of his own mistakes, don't be quick to judge him. His example is not necessarily what you think it is. Instead of saying, "He got what he deserved," feel some compassion for him.

Kindness to Avraham...Avraham imitated Hashem's willingness to go beyond the letter of the law. He did not "owe" itinerant passers-by a meal or a drink, but he gave them willingly and with his full heart. Keep on walking the extra mile!

As He promised to our Fathers...Hashem has a treasury called "*zechut avot*" (the merit of the Fathers). Whenever He is judging His people, He uses the merit of their "fathers" as a source of merit for them. When you come across someone who seems to have almost lost his humanity, force yourself to recall that he is a child of the *Avot*.

As in days of old...Even if a person has totally disassociated himself from the kind of lives that the *Avot* lived, Hashem still recalls that there was at least some time when the person was still innocent and wanted to live a good life. In the same way, if you cannot love someone for who he is, you can try to love him for who he once was.

PRACTICAL PROGRAM FOR COMING CLOSER TO HASHEM

BEGINNING WITH ELUL DAILY:

a) **Give Tzedakah** –Work on your relationship with money to expand yourself (any amount)

b) **Say Tehillim** – Psalm 27 twice a day for 40 days

c) **Make a Cheshbon Nefesh.** Here is how. Buy a notebook and write down the following eras of your life using one page for each era. Then go on to step 1!

My Early Childhood
My Adolescence
My Early Adulthood
The First half of my twenties
The Second half of my twenties
My Thirties
My Forties
My Fifties
My Sixties
My Seventies
My Golden Years (Ad meah ve esrim shanah!)

Step 1

Beginning with the first week, work through your life for about 15-20 minutes a day (maximum). Check off each era as you review it. Remember – no judgment or blame, just focus on what actually occurred.

Step 2

Once you have reviewed your life, revisit each era and examine your responses. Again – no blame or judging.

Write a second check next to each era when you complete this part. You may want to write the responses down in a separate "Cheshbon Nefesh Notebook" to refer to in the future.

Step 3

Review your responses and ask a new question. Put a third check next to each era of your life as you review it.

Which of my responses brought me closer to being the person I want to be?

Which of my responses distanced me from becoming the kind of person I want to be?

Once again – no blame and no judgment. When you made your choices then, you didn't know what you know now. You should have three checks next to each era when you finish this part of the exercise.

Step 4

You are now up to the most important part of your 'Cheshbon Nefesh'. Ask yourself as honestly as you recall, what you were thinking and feeling when you made the decisions that kept you away from your true goals. Write them down.

Don't forget to record the thoughts and feelings that inspired you to make positive choices. It's too easy to be focused on the negative side of your inner life. The positive side is the voice of your soul, and you need to learn to hear it.

You have now made an important discovery about yourself. You know what your core 'middot' are.

20 minutes a day for a week or two during Elul can change your entire sense of who you are, and what you see yourself becoming.

Step 5

Asking forgiveness from people you may have harmed physically, emotionally, spiritually or financially.

As you make your Cheshbon Nefesh, write a list of people to whom you want to speak. Remember that although you may feel embarrassed to admit you are wrong, you are freeing yourself of everything that holds you down. These humiliations may be your ticket to Olam Haba.

Plan what to say before you begin to speak. Focus on restoring your victim's self-esteem.

Consult with a Rav (Rabbi) about any financial compensation you may need to offer.

Step 6

Prepare yourself to forgive others. Reflect on how Hashem determines your fate, for your own good, and how people neither add to nor subtract from what Hashem wants you to experience in life.

Step 7

Now it's time to review the Viduy. Excellent translations are available. Your intent is to say "This is where I was", now I will rid myself of this burden. Saying Viduy should be a spiritual version of getting rid of all the trash.

Step 8

Now that you have focused on your sins, confessed them and want to rid yourself of them, reflect for a moment on how damaging they are to you, so that the likelihood of repeating them will be diminished. This does not mean denying that they felt good at the time. It means recognizing that the loss was far greater than the gain.

Step 9

a) Write your personal 'Plan for the Future'
b) Visualize a better version of the event
c) Identify specific middot
d) Talk to Hashem every day and ask for clarity
e) Make a plan for Elul, for the holidays, for each month and for the entire year. Write it out so that you can refer to it.

Step 10

Whether or not you attend selichot, review the 13 Attributes of Mercy. Ask yourself how you can actually give yourself greater access to your G-dly soul. Try to be as concrete as you can. If it is at all possible to attend selichot, try to do so, as reciting the Attributes of Mercy with a minyan has far greater force than when you reflect upon them at home.

ROSH HASHANAH
PRACTICAL METHODS OF ACCEPTING
THE YOKE OF HEAVEN

Review Before You Go to Shul

Tekia Mindset - Have in mind to want to see both your goodness and Hashem's kavod.

Shevarim Mindset - Envision your will to overcome all the obstacles.

Teruah Mindset - Focus on how you want to see harmony and Mashiach.

1) *Malchuyot*: Bring k'vod Hashem into the world.

2) *Zichronot* (remembrance): Recognizing that nothing is lost, and that Hashem is always loyal to His commitments to us.

3) *Shofarot: Recalling that we all once heard the great shofar at Matan* Torah and will hear it once again when Mashiach comes. Search for your inner memory that actually heard Hashem's voice and yearns to do His will. Be in touch with Bina and Malchut.

ASERET YEMEI TESHUVAH – The Days between RoshHashanah and Yom Kippur:

Make a nightly review of how you are using this time to stretch your spiritual muscles.

YOM KIPPUR – Emerging Cleansed: Ask Hashem to help you become a baal chessed. Each time you say Viduy, affirm that, "this is no longer who I am, or who I want to be."

AFTERWARDS!

Use the beautiful full days between Yom Kippur and Succot to feel the joy of moving forward. Let the days of Succot be ones in which your love and trust in Hashem are concretized.

Throughout the year, review the month before each Rosh Chodesh using our monthly plan, with the final part of your Cheshbon Nefesh statement as your guide.

The day before Rosh Chodesh is called "Yom Kippur Katan", a minor version of Yom Kippur. Make use of this time to redefine the way the past month was, by doing Teshuvah. Some communities even have a special service for Minchah on Erev Rosh Chodesh. Many of the Yom Kippur prayers are recited, including the 13 Attributes of Mercy. If this is not done in your community, or if your schedule doesn't allow for it, don't worry. The main thing is to review the month and do Teshuvah, so that you enter the next month without baggage.

Make each month a month of achievement and joy.

AND FOREVER...

Your cheshbon nefesh should be kept. Next year (and the year after and the year after that) you will be able to see how far you have come. This new stage is called, "Teshuvah on teshuvah", which means that your previous level of self-change no longer satisfies you; you want to make your teshuvah higher, better and more internally integrated.

You can! The day will come,
when you will no longer identify with
thought patterns that once were the real you.
There are no words to fully describe the joy you feel
when you see yourself moving forward
and slowly fulfilling your highest expectations.

Much hatzlachah, and please feel free to share your stories and your progress!

Tziporah Heller
hellersite.contact@gmail.com

GLOSSARY

Adam Harishon – the first man;

ahavat Yisrael – love for every Jew;

Aseret Yemei Teshuvah – the ten days of repentance between Rosh Hashanah and Yom Kippur;

avodah zarah – idol worship;

avon – sin of desire;

baal/baalat Teshuvah – person/people who have returned to Judaism;

bachurim – young Jewish men;

beis medrash – study house;

binah – a form of wisdom/understanding;

brachah – a blessing;

charatah – remorse;

chas v'shalom – G-d forbid;

chazal – our Sages (chachameinu zichronam livracha);

cheirem – excommunication;

cheit – a sin done through negligence;

cheshbon hanefesh – an introspective reckoning;

chessed – loving kindness;

chol Hamo'ed – the interim days of a Jewish holiday;

daven – to pray;

derech – path or direction;

drashah – a speech;

Eretz Yisrael – The Land of Israel;

frum – observant;

ga'avah – haughtiness;

Gadlut/s – greatness

galut/s – exile;

gashmiut – materialism;

Gehennom – a spiritual place of punishment/correction;

Gemara – Rabbinical analysis of the Mishna;

gevurah – the courage to overcome;

halachah – Jewish law;

hallel – prayer of praise;

hashgachah – supervision;

hechsher(–im) – kosher stamp(s) of approval;

ikkar – the main principle;

kaparah – atonement;

kavanah – intention;

kavod – honor;

kedushah – holiness;

Klal Yisrael – the Jewish nation as a whole;

korban – sacrificial gift to G-d;

l'Shem Shamayim – in the Name of Heaven;

lashon hara – badmouthing a fellow Jew;

maamar – a statement;

maariv – the evening service;

machzor(–im) – holiday prayer book(s);

malchut – royalty;

malchuyot – prayers related to G-d's royal status;

Matan Torah – the Giving of the Torah (on Mount Sinai);

mi-d'Oraisa – derived directly from a Biblical source;

middah/middot – personality trait/s;

minchah – the afternoon service;

minyan –quorum of ten men required for Jewish prayer services;

mishnah – redaction of Jewish oral traditions;

mitzvah – a commandment;

mo'ed, mo'adim – appointed time/holidays;

Mashiach – the Redeemer;

mussaf – the additional service;

navi – prophet;

neilah – prayer at the end of Yom Kippur;

nisayon – trial/test/challenge;

nosei avon – He Who carries our sins;

nusach – style of service/prayer/song;

neshamah – soul;

olam habah – the next world;

oveir al pesha – He who overlooks our misdeeds;

passuk – passage of text;

pesha – sin of rebellion;

Rabbeinu Yonah – Yonah ben Abraham Gerondi, also known as Yonah of Gerona, cousin of Nahmanides. He is most famous for his ethical work The Gates of Repentance. (Wikipedia)

rasha – wicked person;

ratzon – will/willpower;

Rosh Hashanah –Jewish New Year;

roshem – indelible impression;

ruchniut – spirituality;

seichel – intelligence/reason;

selichot – penitential prayers;

Shabbat/Shabbos – Sabbath;

shacharit – morning prayer;

shaliach, shelichim – messenger/s;

shalom – peace, sheleimut/s / wholeness;

shekalim – weights/Israeli currency;

Shemoneh Esrei – the "18-part prayer" known also as the Amida;

shidduch – marriage arrangement/partnership;

shiluv – combination;

shofar – ram's horn used for ceremonial blowing;

shofarot – series of blasts blown on the Ram's Horn/prayers relating to the shofar blowing

shoresh – root;

siddur(–im) – Jewish prayer book(s);

simchah – Jewish joy; happy event;

sinat chinam – baseless hatred;

siyatta diShmaya – Heavenly assistance;

Sukkot – Festival of Tabernacles;

ta'avah – desire/lust

tachanun – supplication prayer;

Tanach –abb. Torah, Neviim, Ketuvim (collection of the Torah, Prophets and Writings);

tefillah, tefillot – prayer/s;

tehillah, tehillim – Psalm/s;

teshuvah – return to the path of Torah;

tikkun – correction/repair;

tzaddik – holy individual;

tzedakah – charity/charitable deeds;

viduy – Jewish confessional prayer;

yetzer hara – evil inclination;

yirat Shamayim – fear of Heaven;

Yom Kippur – Day of Atonement;

zikaron/zichronot – remembrance/prayers of recollection;

zivug – partner, mate;

Zohar – (lit. radiance) Kabbalistic treatise.

NOTES

NOTES

NOTES

NOTES

NOTES

NOTES

DAILY VIDEO PROGRAM

As a natural progression to effecting real change,
you can gain from Rebbetzin Heller's Daily Video program.

Few things have changed my life as much as learning Duties of the Heart
- Tziporah Heller

DUTIES OF THE HEART

www.tziporahheller.com

Dear Friends,

*Please join me as we plumb the depths of profound
wisdom in this famed Jewish Literary work,
'Chovot HaLevavot'. Expand your mind and your Jewish
horizons – let it change your life as it has mine.*

Looking forward to learning with you,
Tziporah Heller

Chovot HaLevavot, (Hebrew: חובת הלבבות, Duties of the Heart),
is the primary work of the Jewish philosopher *Bahya ben Joseph ibn Pakuda.*
Ibn Pakuda was a Jewish philosopher and Rabbi who is believed to have lived
in Saragossa, Spain, in the first half of the eleventh century   [Wikipedia]